VIEWS OF 18TH CENTURY CHINA

THE
COSTUME OF CHINA
Inscribed to the
EARL of MACARTNEY. K.B.
Embassador from the
KING of GREAT BRITAIN
to the
EMPEROR of CHINA
A.D. M.DCC.XC.II.
By W: Alexander F.S.A.
Draftsman to the Embassy.

W. Alexander fecit.

London Published Nov.r 1.st 1804 by W. Miller Old Bond Street.

VIEWS OF 18TH CENTURY CHINA
COSTUMES: HISTORY: CUSTOMS

BY
WILLIAM ALEXANDER
AND
GEORGE HENRY MASON

FOREWORD BY
LORD MACLEHOSE OF BEOCH, K.T.
FORMER GOVERNOR OF HONG KONG

STUDIO EDITIONS
LONDON

PUBLISHER'S NOTE

This volume is comprised of two works: *The Costume of China* by George Henry Mason and *The Costume of China* by William Alexander, both of which were printed by William Bulmer and published by William Miller in 1804 and 1805 respectively.

The organization of the plates in this volume is as follows: Plate 1 is by Alexander, Plate 2 by Mason, and the following plates alternate in this fashion up until the last twelve which are all by Mason.

The captions are printed opposite each plate following the format of the original volumes.

This edition published by Studio Editions
An imprint of Bestseller Publications Ltd.
Princess House, 50 Eastcastle Street
London W1N 7AP, England

Copyright © Studio Editions, 1988

ISBN 1-85170-131-1

Printed and bound in Italy
Milanostampa S.p.A.

FOREWORD

In late eighteenth century England *chinoiserie* was in vogue, but knowledge of China was minimal. This book reproduces a very early attempt at a 'documentary'-pictures of people, places, costumes and crafts, with accompanying commentaries published in 1804 and 1805. It has great charm and will be of interest to many readers.

Modern China is very much in the news. Businessmen, financiers, busloads of tourists, media sweep through the country recording their impressions, often of scenes in this books such as the bridge at Suzhou (plate XI). They, and all interested in China, will enjoy the calm of this period piece. It is a reminder of how China appeared through the eyes of travellers in a less hurried age, without benefit of camera, and with plenty of time for each new sight to register.

And, as a period piece, it also starkly reflects many British attitudes to the Chinese of those days, and vice versa. The Collection draws on two separate sources. The enchanting water-colours are by William Alexander, the talented draftsman attached to Lord Macartney's embassy to the Emperor in 1793. He painted the people met and the places passed on the leisurely progress from Tang Gu via Tianjin to Beijing and his return by the Grand Canal to Hagnzhou, Ningbo and Zhoushan where he re-embarked.

He painted most vividly what he saw most of; for instance the two mandarins sent to accompany the embassy (plates I and XXXIX) and whom Macartney liked and respected. Most of the journey was by canal or sea and Alexander is at his best in water scenes such as the canal lock (plate XXIX), or the many paintings of junks and boats. Of course he had the advantage of travelling and painting in comparative comfort. It is said the embassy was "... treated with exquisite hospitality, watched with exquisite vigilance, and dismissed with exquisite courtesy."

The delightful pen and wash pictures of crafts and costumes by Pu Qua were commissioned in Guangzhou by Major Mason who was spending a few months sick leave at the British Factory. They are fascinating in their detail. Most can be enjoyed many times over with some additional item noticed each time.

Until the revolution of 1949 many of these traditional crafts, implements, and methods of carrying them, would have been seen by any visitor to China. Some can be seen today, even perhaps in a back street of Hong Kong. The costume of the "Comedian" (plate LV) can be seen in any Chinese opera.

Mason's Preface is also a period piece in its conscientious curiosity and reflection of how many foreigners saw China—and were seen by Chinese. The notes on individual pictures—Mason's "explanatory letter-press"—were from various sources but including members of Macartney's embassy, though a seam of pure Mason surfaces in many.

The generation of English people who first enjoyed these pictures in the seventeen-nineties and early eighteen hundreds saw China as an exotic and faraway land, but not as "backward" to the West in any general material sense. Nor was it. These pages reflect admiration for Chinese technical contrivance. The technological advances which for a century would give the West such power in comparison to Asia had only just begun at the time of Lord Macartney's mission. What difference would it have made if China had chosen to 'open' to the West much earlier, on the basis of equal treaties and war had never occurred? Whatever the answer, these pictures belong to an era when such a possibility was still conceivable.

MacLehose, Beoch 1988

PREFACE

The very circumscribed limits which are marked out for foreigners at Canton, have rendered the natives of China so completely isolated from the rest of human kind, that only a very superficial acquaintance has been hitherto obtained with the Religion, the Laws, the Manners, or the Arts of a people the most ancient in the discovered world; and it is exceedingly to be regretted, that either habitual caution, ungenerous suspicion, or experienced necessary circumspection, should influence the Chinese, even at the distance of fourteen hundred miles from the capital of their empire, to restrain the observing traveller within his narrow compass.

Insult is the common lot of those foreigners who extend their walk beyond the few yards appointed for their temporary residence. Ill treatment may be expected if they approach the city walls; and either imprisonment or an arrest is the general consequence of passing through its gates. Such, at least, was the situation of foreigners at Canton, at the commencement of the year 1790.[1]

Having suffered the customary verbal abuse from boys and from the common rabble, in their way through the superb streets, and being attended by a vast multitude, on their arrival at the foot of the hill, they were disappointed by their guide refusing to proceed. This produced some strong remonstrances, during which one of the gentlemen slipped through the surrounding crowd, and began to ascend the hill; he was arrested near the summit by two stout natives; two of the party attempting to follow him were intercepted immediately, and a detachment of Tartar soldiers, rushing from a sally-port, carried the first offender within the walls of the city. The remaining gentlemen then used all their rhetoric of signs (for the language on either side was perfectly unintelligible to the other), to obtain a release of the prisoner, or even to be permitted to accompany him, but without effect: a rescue was equally impracticable, and they were compelled into a precipitate retreat amidst the shouts and scurrilities of thousands. It was several hours before the gentleman was released, and then at the intercession of the Hong merchants[2] with the executive power. His treatment had been better than expected, since, with the exception of their repeatedly attempting to snatch his watch, and regarding him with ignorant curiosity, he got home to the Factory, without farther molestation.

This adventure is here related as a convincing proof of the difficulty, if not of the danger, attending inquisitive strangers in China.

The Editor of this Publication, in gratifying his inclination for inquiry, had to surmount the stern impediments above mentioned, united with the infirmity of a constitution impaired in the Carnatic, and for the restoration of which the physician at Madras had prescribed the ineffectual air, as it unfortunately proved in this case, of the south of China.

[1] A party of Englishmen,† on the 24th of December, 1789, had agreed with an old Chinese soldier for a view of the city of Canton—to afford which, he pretended he would conduct them to the top of a considerable eminence‡ that is near the walls of the city, and commands it.

† Consisting of Major Johnson, of the India's Company's Engineers on the Madras establishment; Lieutenant Hardyman, of his Majesty's 36th regiment; and his brother Lucius, then a midshipman in the British navy; Captain Hervey, from Calcutta; Doctor Truston; and Lieutenant Mason, the Editor of this Work, at that time in the 36th regiment, and Major of Brigade to his Majesty's forces on the coast of Coromandel.

‡ Called, by Europeans, Padrè Hill.

[2] A company of Chinese merchants, by whom all the immense commerce at Canton is regulated.

From the attentive hospitality of some of the gentlemen then residing at the British factory[1] the Editor received, during a stay of several months, important information. Under the auspices of those gentlemen, he partook of several entertainments given by the Hong merchants at their own houses; from which advantages, with the aid of some donations, unwearied diligence, and frequent exertions of patience, he obtained no very inconsiderable knowledge of the Chinese customs.

The Chinese, collectively, appear to be ingenious in their peaceful arts; polished and courteous in their manners; moral and sagacious in their civil institutes; just and polite in their penal laws; and in want of nothing but the Blessing of Revealed Religion to render them one of the happiest people in the universe.

For the better information of his friends in Europe, the Editor obtained correct drawings of the Chinese in their respective habits and occupations; the itinerant mechanics and handicraftsmen, in particular; fac-similes of which are exhibited on the subsequent pages. Not intended, originally, for public inspection, they are thus, at the instance of some learned and ingenious friends, issued from his portfolio after ten years privacy; and it is presumed, that partial instruction, and general amusement, must result from such accurate representations of the domestic and mechanical habits of an original and remote nation, which, though discovered upwards of five hundred years,[2] is still but little known by Europeans.

In order to render this purpose effectual, it was absolutely necessary to attach a few lines of explanatory letter-press to each plate, and wherever the recollection of the Editor is deficient, he has repaired it by careful selections from the narratives of almost every traveller from Nieuhoff and Navarette to Saunton and Van Braam. Hence the man of reading will find various circumstances advanced by those writers, corroborated by these evidences.

It may be necessary that the Editor should disavow his having arrogated any pretension to be esteemed the historian of the Chinese nation. He has already stated the motive of the undertaking, and acknowledged that much of the letter-press is composed of opposite quotations, which he has not considered it necessary to mark, more especially as it would have disfigured the text; and as the references would have encumbered the margins.

In these miscellaneous descriptions, men of genius and learning will, with their accustomed candour, allow for the inaccuracies of one who, from his early youth, has been devoted to a profession which generally militates against literary improvement.

Lastly, The Editor would deem himself deficient in gratitude if he concluded this address without acknowledging his obligations to the liberal and discerning few, who, upon receiving his plan for publishing this volume, readily patronised the undertaking at its outset, and have continued their encouragement to its conclusion.

Nass House, Gloucestershire.
May 4, 1800.

---

[1] Particularly William Fitzhugh, James Drummond, and Thomas Fitzhugh, Esquires.

[2] A. D. 1295. The first accounts of China was brought into Europe by Marco Polo, a Venetian, who had travelled into that country through Tartary.

PLATE I

PORTRAIT OF VAN-TA-ZHIN

A military Mandarine (or Nobleman) of China

This officer (a colleague of Chow-ta-zhin, who was a mandarine of the civil department) was appointed by the Emperor to attend the British Embassy, from the time of its arrival in the gulf of Pe-tchi-li, till its departure from Canton. Van-ta-zhin was a man of a bold, generous, and amiable character, and possessed of qualifications eminently suited to his profession, being well skilled in the use of the bow, and in the management of the sabre. For services performed in the wars of Thibet, he wore appended from his cap, a peacock's feather, as an extraordinary mark of favour from his sovereign, besides a red globe of coral which distinguished his rank. He is represented in his usual, or undress, consisting of a short loose jacket of fine cotton, and an under vest of embroidered silk; from his girdle hangs suspended his handkerchief, his knife and chopsticks* in a case, and purses for tobacco: on his thumbs are two broad rings of agate, for the purpose of drawing the bowstring. The heads of the arrows, which are thrust into the quiver, are variously pointed, as barbed, lozenge-headed, &c. His boots are of satin, with thick soles of paper: these are always worn by the mandarines and superior Chinese.

* Quoit-zau, or Chopsticks, are used in China instead of forks; they are two round slender sticks of ivory, ebony, &c. and used in the manner of pincers.

W. Alexander delt.

London, Published July 20th 1797, by G. Nicol, Pall mall.

PLATE II

A MANDARIN OF DISTINCTION

In his Habit of Ceremony

The dress of a Chinese is suited to the gravity of his demeanor. It consists, in general, of a long vest extending to the ankle: the sleeves are wide at the shoulder, are gradually narrower at the wrist, and are rounded off in the form of a horse-shoe, covering the whole hand when it is not lifted up. No man of rank is allowed to appear in public without boots, which have no heels, and are made of satin, silk, or calico. In full dress he wears a long silk gown, generally of a blue colour and heavily embroidered; over this is placed a sur-coat of silk, which reaches to the hand, and descends below the knee. From his neck is suspended a string of costly coral beads. His cap is edged with satin, velvet, or fur, and on the crown is a red ball, with a peacock's feather hanging from it: these are badges of distinction conferred by the emperor. The embroidered bird upon the breast is worn only by mandarins high in civil rank, while the military mandarins are distinguished by an embroidered dragon. All colours are not suffered to be worn indiscriminately. The emperor and the princes of the blood only, are allowed to wear yellow; although violet colour is sometimes chosen by mandarins of rank on days of ceremony. The common people seldom wear any other than blue or black, and white is universally adopted for mourning.—The Chinese carefully avoid every word or gesture which may betray either anger or any violent emotion of the mind. They entertain the highest reverence for their parents, and respect for the aged. They are enthusiastic admirers of virtue, and venerate the memory of such of their nation as have been celebrated for a love of justice and of their country. With this singular people neither riches nor birth can ever establish the smallest claim to honours. Personal merit is the sole basis upon which any man can raise himself to distinguished rank. Talents and virtue are indispensably requisite for those in power; and where they are deficient, every advantitious or hereditary pretension is totally disallowed.

Qua. Canton. Delin.

Dadley. London. Sc.

Published May 4. 1799 by W. Miller. Old Bond Street. London.

PLATE III

A PAGODA (OR TOWER)

Near the City of Sou-tcheou

These buildings are a striking feature on the face of the country. The Chinese name for them is Ta; but Europeans have improperly denominated them Pagodas, a term used in some Oriental countries for a temple of religious worship. It seems the Ta of China is not intended for sacred purposes, but erected occasionally by viceroys or rich mandarines, either for the gratification of personal vanity, or with the idea of transmitting a name to posterity; or perhaps built by the magistracy merely as objects to enrich the landscape.

They are generally built of brick, and sometimes cased with porcelain, and chiefly consist of nine, though some have only seven or five stories, each having a gallery, which may be entered from the windows, and a projecting roof, covered with tiles of a rich yellow colour, highly glazed, which receive from the sun a splendour equal to burnished gold. At each angle of the roofs a light bell is suspended, which is rung by the force of the wind, and produces a jingling not altogether unpleasant. These buildings are for the most part octagonal, though some few are hexagonal, and round. They diminish gradually in circumstance from the foundation to the summit, and have a staircase within, by which they ascend to the upper story. In height they are generally from an hundred to an hundred and fifty feet, and are situated indiscriminately on eminences or plains, or oftener in cities. The Print represents one of modern structure. Those of a more ancient date are in a mutilated state, and the roofs covered with grey tiles, overgrown with moss, while others have a cornice only instead of the projecting roof.

Vide the print of Lin-tsin Pagoda in Sir George Staunton's Account of the Chinese Embassy.

London Publish'd July 26. 1797. by G. Nicol. Pallmall.

PLATE IV

A WATCHMAN

At the approach of night, the gates of the cities in China, and the barricades at the end of each street, are carefully shut. During the night no persons of credit are seen in the streets, which abound with watchmen, who strike upon a piece of bamboo in their left hand, to denote the time and to mark their own vigilance. Those whom they meet in their walk are questioned, and if the reply be satisfactory, they are permitted to pass through a wicket in the barricade. The watchmen carry lanterns, upon which are written their names and the district to which they belong. In the very hot months, all the lower classes of Chinese have their feet and legs bare.

Qua. Canton. Delin.

Dadley. London. Sculp.

Published May 4 1799 by W. Miller Old Bond Street, London.

PLATE V

THE TRAVELLING BARGE

Of Van-ta-zhin

As travelling in China is generally performed on the water, a prodigious number of Yachts or Barges of various forms are employed, as well for that purpose, as for the conveyance of merchandize.

The central apartment, which has an awning over the windows, is occupied by the proprietor; the fore part of the vessel by his servants, and the aft or stern part is used for culinary purposes, and sleeping places for the boatmen. Barges of this kind have one large sail of matting, stretched out by bamboos, running horizontally across it; the sail may be instantly taken in by letting go the haulyards, when the sail falls in folds similar to a fan. When the wind or tide is unfavourable, these vessels are either tracked along by human labour, or sculled by large oars which work on pivots at the bows and stern: by means of these oars, which are never taken out of the water, but simply sculled to and fro, the vessel is impelled onwards with considerable rapidity. The triple umbrella proclaims a Mandarine of consequence to be on board. The large lanterns with Chinese characters on them, and the ensign at the stern, are likewise marks of distinction.

London. Publish'd July 20. 1797. by G. Nicol. Pallmall.

PLATE VI

A WOMAN MAKING STOCKINGS

The men's stockings are made of stuff, stitched and lined with cotton, with a line of gold thread sewed along the top. These stockings are somewhat misshapen, but are very warm.—There is an engaging modesty in the Chinese habit which adorns every class in life. The dress of the women is fastened close round the throat, their sleeves conceal their hands, and they wear long drawers reaching to their ankles. Those who can afford it, purchase earrings of gold, and large armlets of the same metal.—The hair of the Chinese is universally black. The women comb it up very nicely, and braid or coil it on the head with much neatness; sometimes it is fastened with a gold bodkin or two, and generally ornamented with natural or artificial flowers, disposed according to the fancy of the wearer. The young and unmarried are required by custom to wear their hair combed over their foreheads, whilst the eye-brows of both are trimmed into a mere pencil line.—None but the lowest orders of Chinese women are indulged with the natural use of their feet. The parents or nurses of a female infant of superior condition carefully fold the toes under the feet, the great one excepted; and by being confined thus, they are rendered incapable of ever recovering their natural shape and position. The motive for this singular distortion is not acknowledged by any of the natives, neither is it easy to be surmised. If the custom proceeded from a notion of rendering the women more usefully domestic, the purpose is in a great measure defeated, since they are by this practice deprived of that active power which is necessary for the performance of domestic duties. If it be from a distrust of their fidelity, it is remarkable that no such custom prevails amongst the Turks, or other Asiatics, who are equally jealous of their women. It seems probable, that, either from habit or prejudice, they attach ideas of vulgarity and disgust to this part of the human frame. The Chinese ladies are ridiculed by the European nations on account of this deformity, which is the result of fashion only, whilst they do not consider, that, unsightly as it may be, it is perfectly consistent with those peculiar principles of modesty and decorum which the Chinese profess.

Pu Qua, Canton, Delin.   Dadley, London, Sculp.

Published May 4, 1799, by W. Miller, Old Bond Street, London.

PLATE VII

A CHINESE SOLDIER OF INFANTRY

Or Tiger of War

The dress of the Chinese is generally loose; the soldiers of this part of the army, with few exceptions, are the only natives whose close habit discovers the formation of the limbs.

The general uniform of the Chinese troops is cumbrous and inconvenient; this of the Tiger of War, is much better adapted for military action.

The Missionaries have denominated them TIGERS of War, from their dress, which has some resemblance to that animal; being striped, and having ears on the cap.

They are armed with a scimitar of rude workmanship, and a shield of wicker or basket-work, so well manufactured, as to resist the heaviest blow from a sword. On it is painted the face of an imaginary monster, which (like that of Medusa) is supposed to possess the power of petrifying the beholder.

At a distance is seen a Military Post, with the Imperial flag, which is yellow, hoisted near it.

W.Alexander. fecit.

London. Publish'd. October 12.th 1797. by G. Nicol, Pall mall.

PLATE VIII

A MONEY-CHANGER

He is examining a dollar, for which he gives a number of the pieces of copper-money, which are placed before him, according to the current exchange. This coin is round, somewhat larger and thinner than the English farthing, having a square hole in the middle; and is marked with the dynasty in which it was struck: it is, in fact, the only currency, and is used separately for small change, or strung, as here represented, by hundreds, fifties, &c. forming what they call "candareens" and "maces," sums of nominal value. The instrument in his right-hand is employed to cut the dollar, should he doubt its worth. The Chinese money is never stamped with the head of the prince, because they deem it disrespectful to the majesty of the emperor, that his image should be perpetually passing through the hands of dealers and the dregs of the people.

Pu-Qua, Canton, Delin.

Dadley, London, Sculp.

Published May 4, 1799, by W. Miller, Old Bond Street, London.

PLATE IX

A GROUP OF TRACKERS

Of the Vessels, at Dinner

When the wind or tide is unfavourable to the progress of the vessels, the sail and oars are laid aside, and the more general mode of tracking them is adopted. The number of trackers employed, depends on the size of the vessel, or strength of the current, which often requires the efforts of twenty men to counteract: these are kept in full exertion by a task-master, who most liberally applies the whip, where he sees a disposition to idleness.

The chief food of these poor labourers, is rice; and they consider it a luxury, when they can procure vegetables fried in rancid oil, or animal offal, to mix with it. They are represented cooking their meal over an earthen stove; the standing figure is employed eating his rice in the usual way, which is by placing the edge of the bowl against his lower lip, and with the chopsticks knocking the contents into his mouth.

They sometimes wear shoes made of straw, but are more frequently without any. The pien-za, or queue, is often inconvenient to Chinese labourers; to avoid which they twist it round their heads, and secure it by tucking in its extremity.

The flat boards, with cordage to them, are applied to the breast when dragging the junks, or vessels.

London, Published Oct.r 12 1797. by G. Nicol Pall mall.

PLATE X

A BARBER

Many of the following plates represent itinerant traders and mech-anics, who carry on their shoulders their articles for sale, or the implements of their occupation, balanced at the extremities of a bamboo lath. This lath is light, strong, and elastic. When one shoulder is fatigued, they have a method of dexterously swinging the lath round the back of the head to the opposite shoulder. From history we learn that the Chinese were not originally used to shave their heads; but that the Tartar princes, when they conquered China, though they continued the former constitution, manners, and laws, compelled the subdued nation to adopt their form of dress. This custom was enforced by the political motive of doing away every recollection of their subjugation. There is now no difference in the form of wearing the hair, between the emperor and the lowest mechanic. The head is entirely shaven, excepting the middle of the back part, from whence the hair hangs as long as it will grow. It is neatly braided, and tied together at the extremities with a small riband. The lower sort of people frequently coil their hair round the top of their head, to prevent it from dangling in their way. The Chinese barber performs very dexterously upon the spot, whether in the open street or elsewhere. He shaves the head, cleans the ears, sets the eye-brows in order, and shampoes (a custom universally practised in Asia; which consists in stretching, rubbing, and gently beating the limbs and muscles, in order to promote a quicker circulation of the blood;) all which services he executes for a few pieces of copper coin. The little drawers contain his instruments, and serve for a seat upon which his customer is placed: the counterpoise is a large piece of bamboo, holding water, over which are seen his razor-strap and napkin.

Pu-Qua, Canton, Delin.

Dadley, London, Sculp.

Published May 4, 1799, by W. Miller, Old Bond Street, London.

PLATE XI

VIEW OF A BRIDGE

In the Environs of the City of Sou-tcheou

The Bridges of China are variously constructed. There are many of three arches, some of which are very light, and elegant; others are simply pyramidal piers, with timbers and flooring laid horizontally across them.

This arch, which resembles the outline of a horseshoe, occurred very frequently in the route of a part of the Embassy from Han-tcheou to Chusan. Like most of the Chinese bridges, it is of quick ascent, making an angle of full twenty degrees with the horizon, and is ascended by steps. The carriage of merchandize by land, is therefore inconsiderable; the rivers and canals being the high roads of China.

The material of which these bridges are composed, is a species of coarse marble. The projecting stones and uprights against the surface, are supposed to strengthen or bind the fabric; and the five circular badges over the arch, contain Chinese characters, which may probably shew the name of the architect, and date of its erection.

The temporary ornament over the centre of the arch, consisting of upright poles, painted and adorned with silken streamers, and suspended lanterns, was erected in compliment to the Embassador. The six soldiers from an adjacent Military Post, was likewise ordered to stand on the bridge by way of salute.

W. Alexander fecit.

London. Publish'd Oct.r 12. 1797. by G. Nicol, Pallmall.

PLATE XII

A BOOKSELLER

The Chinese have practised the art of printing from time immemorial; but they use no press as the Europeans do. They carve their letters upon blocks of wood; and their paper being very thin and transparent, will bear printing only on one side: hence every leaf is doubled, the fold being at the edge. They cover their books with a neat sort of pasteboard, of a grey colour; or else with fine satin, or flowered silk. Some are bound with red brocade, interspersed with gold and silver flowers, a manner of binding extremely neat and ornamental. Their books are lettered upon the cover.

The common people have ballads and songs, inculcating chiefly the rules of civility, the relative duties of life, and the maxims of morality. The Chinese novels are amusing and instructive; they enliven the imagination without corrupting the heart, and are replete with axioms which tend to the reformation of manners, by a powerful recommendation of the practice of virtue. Conscious that the political existence of a government depends on the proper regulation of the impulses of nature, the severest penalties are denounced by the Chinese code of laws against all publications unfriendly to decency and good order: the purchasers of them are held in detestation by the greater part of the community, and, with the publishers, are alike obnoxious to the laws, which no rank or station, however exalted, can violate with impunity. The greatest encouragement is given by this extraordinary people to the cultivation of letters. The literati rank above the military, are eligible to the highest stations, and receive the most profound homage from all ranks.

The Chinese has no resemblance to any other dead or living language: all others have an alphabet, the letters of which, by their various combinations, form syllables and words; whereas this has no alphabet, but as many characters and different figures as there are words and changes.

Some of the Chinese paper is made of cotton, some of hemp; other sorts are of bamboo, of the mulberry, or of the arbutus, which latter is most in use. The inner rind being reduced by maceration and pounding to a fluid paste, is then placed in frame moulds, and the sheets are completed by drying in a sort of stove.

The ink, commonly called "Indian ink," is made of lamp-black, beat up in a mortar with musk, and a thin size. When brought to the consistence of paste, it is put into small moulds, stamping upon the ink what characters or figures are wanted; and it is then dried in the sun or air.

The Chinese do not use pens, but pencils made with hair, particularly with that of the rabbit. When they write, they have upon their table a small piece of polished marble, with a hollow at one end to contain water; into this they dip their stick of ink, and rub it upon the smooth part, leaning more or less heavily, to proportion the blackness. When they write, they hold the pencil perpendicularly. They write in columns, from the top of the paper to the bottom, commencing on the right-hand side of the margin, and end their books where Europeans begin theirs, whose last page is with them the first.

The paper, ink, pencil, and marble, are called "Paut-see," or, "The four precious things."

Pu-Qua, Canton, Delin.

Dadley, London, Sculp.

Published, May 4.1799 by W. Miller, Old Bond Street, London.

PLATE XIII

PORTRAIT OF A TRADING SHIP

These ships venture as far as Manilla, Japan, and even Batavia, which is the most distant port they visit; and many of them are from eight hundred to a thousand tons burthen. In these voyages the mariners take the moderate season of the year, and though well acquainted with the use of the compass, generally keep near the coast.

No alteration has been made in the naval architecture of China for many centuries past. The Chinese are so averse to innovation, and so attached to ancient prejudices, that although Canton is annually frequented by the ships of various European nations, whose superiority of construction they must acknowledge, yet they reject any improvement in their vessels.

The stern of this ship falls in with an angle; other vessels are formed with a cavity, in which the rudder is defended from the violence of the sea; yet this contrivance certainly subjects the ship to much hazard, when running before the wind in high seas.

On each bow is painted an eye, with the pupil turned forwards; perhaps with the idea of keeping up some resemblance to a fish; or from a superstitious notion, that the ship may thus see before her, and avoid danger.

The ports often serve as windows, not many of them being furnished with ordnance.

London Published Oct.ʳ 12.ᵗʰ 1797. by G. Nicol, Pallmall.

W. Alexander fecit.

PLATE XIV

A FROG-CATCHER

The lower sort of people in China are not delicate in their eating; they do not scruple to feed heartily upon animals which die a natural death, as is noticed by several voyagers. The poor eat frogs and rats, dried hams, of which latter are exposed to sale in the streets; and the middling sort think a young dog no bad food.—This seems to have been a delicacy of very ancient date. The Romans, according to Pliny,* considered sucking puppies as an excellent dish.

They have a method of taking frogs in China, during the night, by means of fire, which is carried in a wire net, as represented in this plate.

* Plin. Nat. Hist. lib. xxix. cap. 14.—"Catulos lactantes adeo puros existimabant ad cibum "ut etiam placandis numinibus hostiarum vice uterentur his."—It appears likewise from Athenæus, lib. v. page 281, and from Galen, lib. iii. de Alimentis, cap. 2, that the Greeks ate the flesh of young dogs as a delicacy.

Pu-Qua, Canton, Delin.

Dadley, London, Sculp.

Published May 4, 1799, by W. Miller, Old Bond Street, London.

PLATE XV

PORTRAIT OF THE PURVEYOR

For the Embassy, while the Embassador remained at Macao

The dress of this figure is the same as is generally worn by the citizens, or middle class of people in China, with variations in the colour; and some difference of form in hats, caps, boots, &c. &c.

The external jacket is of sheep skin, ornamented with crescents of the same material, dyed of another colour, sewed into it at equal distances; and has a collar of sable, or fox skin. This surtout is worn on such mornings and evenings as are fresh and cold; in the day time (if found inconveniently hot) it is laid aside. Under this is worn a vest of figured silk; beneath which is another of white linen, or taffeta; and lastly, a pair of loose drawers: in the summer season these are of linen or silk, and for the winter, they are lined with fur, or quilted with raw silk; and in the northern provinces they are worn, made of skins only.

The cap is composed of a coarse sort of felt, which is very common; and while new, they have the shape of those worn by the Mandarins, (see the Portrait of Van-ta-zhin), but they soon become pliant and misshapen, by wear, or when rain has taken the stiffness from them. The stockings are of nankeen, quilted on the inside with cotton. The shoes are likewise nankeen, with thick soles made of paper.

From the girdle on the right side, hangs a flint and steel, and knife sheath; on the left, purses for tobacco, or snuff.

The box held in his hand contains sweetmeats; a jar of which he entreated the persons of the Embassy to accept as a token of his regard.

The back ground, is a scene at Macao.

PLATE XVI

A PORK-BUTCHER

The butcher represented in this plate, carries his meat in a basket, suspended from one end of the bamboo lath, which is counterpoised at the other end by his chopping-block, wherein there is a drawer to hold his knives, &c. On the basket may be observed a steel-yard (if the expression be allowable) made of wood, and graduated according to Chinese avoirdupois.

The Chinese prefer the flesh of swine to that of all other animals: it is much better than in Europe, and their hams are particularly excellent.

Pu-Quà Cantòn, Delin.

Dadley. London. Sculp.ͭ

Published May 4. 1799. by W. Miller. Old Bond Street. London.

PLATE XVII

PUNISHMENT OF THE CANGUE

By which name it is commonly known to Europeans, but by the Chinese called the Tcha; being a heavy tablet, or collar of wood, with a hole through the centre, or rather two pieces of wood hollowed in the middle which inclose the neck (similar to our pillory), there are, likewise, two other holes, for the hands of the delinquent, who is sometimes so far favoured as to have but one hand confined; by which indulgence he is enabled with the other to lessen the weight on his shoulders.

The division in the Cangue which receives the head, is kept together by pegs, and is further secured by a slip of paper pasted over the joint, on which is affixed the seal, or chop, of the Mandarin; and the cause of punishment likewise depicted on it, in large characters.

The weight of these ignominious machines, which are from sixty to two hundred pounds in weight, and the time criminals are sentenced to endure them, depends on the magnitude of the offence, being sometimes extended, without intermission, to the space of one, two, or even three months; during which time the offender's nights are spent in the prison, and in the morning he is brought by the magistrates' assistant, led by a chain, to a gate of the city, or any place most frequented; when the attendant suffers him to rest his burthen against a wall, where he remains exposed throughout the day to the derision of the populace, without the means of taking food but by assistance. Nor is the punishment at an end when the Mandarin has ordered him to be released from the Cangue; a certain number of blows from the bamboo, remain to be inflicted; for which chastisement, in the most abject manner, with forehead to the earth, he thanks the Mandarin for his fatherly correction.

London Published May 1st 1798. by G. Nicol, Pall mall.

PLATE XVIII

A BONZEE BEGGING ALMS

This represents a priest attached to the worship of Fò, a deity, who has more followers than any other in China. From him is supposed to have sprung the very ancient doctrine of the transmigration of souls. This sect pay their adorations to an infinite number of animals, on the supposition that the soul of their deity might, in its numerous metamorphoses, have animated such bodies. They also believe, that by the mere pronunciation of the name of their favourite deity they shall be exonerated from their sins. The bonzees go from door to door, chaunting a sort of hymn, which they accompany with gentle taps upon a hollow piece of wood, formed somewhat like a pear. They go closely shaven and bare-headed, and beg in the most supplicating posture; yet zeal for the service of their deity does not prevent them from guarding against the severities their flesh would otherwise be subject to from frequent genuflexions: upon each knee is fastened a pad of calico, thickly quilted with cotton. A painted board is tied upon their backs, bearing characters which denote their sect, and the temple to which they are attached. The Chinese have likewise their household deities, the worship and influence of which bear a striking analogy to the Penates of the ancient Romans.

Many Catholic princes sent jesuits and other missionaries in order to introduce the Christian religion in China, and it is pretended that this mission took place as early as the year 1636. It is said that Lewis XV. of France, expended annually 9200 livres for their support. The missionaries from the court of Rome endeavoured to encroach on the civil institutions at Pekin, which induced the emperor Quang-Hi to banish them from his dominions.

Pa-Qua. Canton. Delin.

Dadley. London. Sculp.

Published May 4. 1799. by W. Miller, Old Bond Street, London.

PLATE XIX

SOUTH GATE OF THE CITY OF TING-HAI

In the Harbour of Tchu-san

The Port of Tchu-san, into which the English were formerly admitted, lies in latitude, thirty degrees and twenty minutes north, or about mid-way, on the east coast of China, between Can-ton and Pe-king.

The walls inclosing this city are near thirty feet in height, which (excepting Pagodas, public buildings, &c.) entirely preclude the sight of the houses, which in general have but one story.

The bricks and tiles of China, either from a different quality of the substance that composes them, or from being dried and burnt in a different manner, are of a bluish, or slate colour. The embrasures have no artillery, but there are loop-holes in the merlons for the use of archers. On the walls, and at the entrance of the gate, are tents as guard-houses, where a sufficient number of soldiers are continually stationed. At an early hour of the night the gates are shut, after which, no person can be admitted on any pretence whatever.

The angles of the roofs which curve upwards, and project considerably, in Chinese buildings, most likely have their origin from tents; for a canvas resting on four cords would receive the same form. The ridges on the angles of the buildings over the gate are decorated with figures of animals, dragons, &c.; and the sides of the building, and extremities of the beams, painted with various colours. The yellow board over the arch has Chinese characters on it; which probably signify the name and rank of the city. The carriage entering the city, is a vehicle used in common with sedans, for the conveyance of persons of consequence. The Chinese have not adopted the use of springs, therefore these machines are little better than a European cart. The nearest figure shews the usual method of carrying light burthens, as vegetables, fruit, &c. &c.

London Publish'd May 1.st 1798, by G. Nicol Pall mall.

PLATE XX

A MAN WITH A RAREE-SHOW

Whether the Europeans borrowed the idea from the Chinese, or were the inventors of this puerile object of curiosity, cannot easily be decided; the similarity of this harmless amusement will be obvious to every one. The Chinese showman produces a succession of pictures to the perspective glass, by means of small strings, and relates a story and description of each subject as he presents it.

Pu-Qüa, Canton, Delin.

Dadley, London, Sculp.

Published May 4.1799, by W. Miller, Old Bond Street, London.

PLATE XXI

THREE VESSELS LYING AT ANCHOR

In the River of Ning-po

The middle vessel, with the stern in view, was a trading ship without cargo; in this the peculiar construction of the stern is exemplified, being hollowed into an indented angle, for the protection of the rudder, which is lifted out of the water by a rope, to preserve it. The Chinese characters over the rudder, denote the name of the vessel; and the bisected cone against the stern, is appropriated to the same use as the quarter-galleries of our ships.

The small vessel was hired for the service of the Embassy, and employed in transporting baggage; the larger vessel conveyed a part of the Embassy from Ning-po, to Tchu-san, where they embarked on board the Hindostan, for Can-ton. The prow of this vessel has a singular appearance, the upper part of the stern terminating in two wings, or horns. The small boat (or Sam-paan, as called by the Chinese) is a necessary appendage to vessels of this size.

W. Alexander fecit.

London. Publish'd, May 1st 1798. by G. Nicol. Pallmall.

PLATE XXII

A CHINESE WOMAN

This woman appears to be of middle age, and by her ornaments and feet rather above the common rank. The diminutiveness of the latter compels her to move with such a cautious and unsteady step as causes a painful sensation to an European. In her right hand is a fan or parasol; in her left an artificial flower.

Pa-Qua. Canton. Delin.

Dadley. London. Sculp.

Published May 4.1799. by W. Miller. Old Bond Street. London.

PLATE XXIII

PORTRAIT OF A LAMA OR BONZE

The priesthood of China and Tartary are, since the conquest of the former, become nearly the same, in respect to manners, dress, &c.; and these are the only people of either nation, who have the head shaved entirely. Their general habit is a loose robe or gown, with a broad collar of silk or velvet; the colour of the robe depending on the particular sect or monastery to which they belong. Some of them wear an ornament resembling a cap, exquisitely wrought in wood, &c. which they affix to the back of the head.

This figure is from one of the Lamas inhabiting the temple called Poo-ta-la, which is situated near the Imperial residence at Zhe-hol in Tartary. These Priests are all clad in the royal colour, yellow; their hats have very broad brims, answering the double purpose of defence from sun and rain, and are neatly manufactured from straw and split bamboo.

The temple Poo-ta-la, which is distantly seen, maintains eight hundred Lamas, devoted to the worship of the deity Fo: to this sect the Emperor is attached, and it is the general religion of the empire. The form of this edifice is square, with lesser buildings in the Chinese style of architecture adjoining: each side of the large building measures two hundred feet, and is nearly of the same height, having eleven rows of windows. In the centre of this immense fabric is a chapel, profusely decorated and roofed with tiles of solid gold. Within this chapel is the sanctum sanctorum, containing statues of the idol Fo, with his wife and child.

London Publishd. Sepr. 1st 1798. by G. Nicol Pallmall.

W. Alexander fecit.

PLATE XXIV

A PIPE-SELLER

The body of a Chinese pipe is always of a sort of bamboo reed, and generally black. The bowls and the mouth-pieces (which this figure has for sale in his left hand) are of white copper; these are taken off or put on at pleasure. Small pouches, which contain the tobacco, are suspended by a silken string from about the centre of the pipes. These little pouches are chiefly of satin, and are very neatly embroidered with flowers.

Pu-Qua, Canton, Delin.

Dadley, London, Sculp!

Published May 4.1799. by W. Miller Old Bond Street London.

PLATE XXV

A CHINESE LADY AND HER SON

attended by a Servant

The female sex in China, live retired in proportion to their situation in life. The lower orders are not more domesticated than in Europe; but the middle class are not often seen from home, and ladies of rank scarcely ever. Alterations of dress are never made from caprice or fashion; the season of the year, and disposing the various ornaments, making the only difference. Instead of linen, the ladies substitute silk netting; over which is worn an under vest and drawers of taffeta; and, (should the weather require no additional covering,) they have for the external garment, a long robe of silk or satin, richly embroidered. Great care is taken in ornamenting the head: the hair, after being smoothed with oil and closely twisted, is brought to the crown of the head, and fastened with bodkins of gold and silver; across the forehead is a band, from which descends a peak of velvet, decorated with a diamond or pearl, and artificial flowers, are fancifully arranged on each side of the head. Ear-rings, and the string of perfumed beads suspended from the shoulder, likewise make up part of the ornaments of dress. The use of cosmetics is well known among the ladies of China; painting the face both white and red, is in common practice with them: they place a decided red spot on the lower lip, and the eyebrows are brought by art to be very narrow, black, and arched.

Their small shoes are elegantly wrought, and the contour of the ankles are never seen, by reason of the loose bandage round them. Boys, till about seven years of age, frequently have two queues, encouraged to grow from each side of the head. The servant, as is usual with the lower class, wears on the wrist a ring of brass or tutenag.

W. Alexander fecit.

London Published Sep.ᵗ 1.ˢᵗ 1798. by G. Nicol Pallmall.

PLATE XXVI

A TAMBOURINER

The Chinese have various instruments of the drum kind; but there is none which admits so much display of action and of antic as the tambourine, wherein they are not rivalled by any performers in Europe.

Pu-Qua, Canton, Delin.

Dadley, London, Sculpt.

Published May 4 1799 by W. Miller, Old Bond Street, London.

PLATE XXVII

VIEW OF A BURYING-PLACE

near Han-tcheou-fou

The tombs and monuments of China exhibit a variety of architecture, except those of the common people, which are nothing more than small cones of earth, on the summits of which they frequently plant dwarf trees. These simple graves are occasionally visited by the family, who are particularly careful to trim and keep them in neat order.

The coffins of this country are made of very thick boards, plentifully pitched within, and varnished without; which makes them durable, and prevents them from emitting putrid exhalations: this process being absolutely necessary, where the coffins of the lower class often lie scattered among the tombs, totally uncovered with earth.

The rich spare no expense in having coffins of the most precious wood, which are frequently provided several years before the death of the persons intending to occupy them. A deceased parent is oftentimes preserved in the house by an affectionate family for months, and even years; yet, either from their knowledge of embalming, or from the practice of securing the joints of the coffin with bitumen, no contagious effluvia proceeds from it.

The duty of the widow or children is not finished here: even after the corpse is deposited in the sepulchre of its ancestors, the disconsolate relatives (clad in coarse canvas) still reside with the body, and continue their lamentations for some months. The characters on the monuments, signify the name and quality of the defunct; and epitaphs, extolling the virtues of the deceased, are inscribed on tablets of marble at the entrance of the vaults. The tomb with steps before it, and another, inclosed with cypresses, are common with people of affluence.

W. Alexander fecit.

London Publish'd Sep.t 1.st 1798 by G. Nicol Pallmall.

PLATE XXVIII

A BEGGAR WITH A DOG

In a country containing upwards of three hundred millions of inhabitants, it may be imagined that some individuals subsist upon the precarious bounty of the charitable.

This plate, as also three others, exhibit a variety of wretchedness, and are correct representations of the Chinese mendicants, who practise many tricks and austerities in order to extort alms.

The one here represented is attended by a dog, which is taught to tread upon the end of a light board, that, acting as a lever, raises a stone fastened to the opposite end. This stone then falls into a small wooden cup, and thus affords, in miniature, a representation of the mode of beating out rice from the husk. The man receives his alms in a wicker dish.

Pu-Qua, Canton, Delin.

Dadley, London, Sculp.

Published May 4 1799 by W. Miller, Old Bond Street, London.

PLATE XXIX

FRONT VIEW OF A BOAT

passing over an inclined Plane or Glacis

In the passage from Han-tcheou-fou to Tchu-san (which was the route of part of the Embassy), the face of the country is mountainous; therefore the communication of the canals is continued by means of this sort of locks, two of which were passed over on the 16th of November, 1793.

In this subject, the difference of level between the two canals was full six feet; in the higher one, the water was within one foot of the upper edge of the beam over which the boat passes. The machinery consisted of a double glacis of sloping masonary, with an inclination of about forty degrees from the horizon. The boats are drawn over by capstans, two of which are generally sufficient, though sometimes four or six are required for those of greater burthen; in this case, there are holes in the ground to receive them. When a boat is ready to pass over, the ropes from the capstans (which have a loop at their extremities) are brought to the stern of the vessel; one loop is then passed through the other, and a billet of wood thrust into the noose, to prevent their separation; the projecting gunwale at the same time keeping the ropes in a proper situation. This being adjusted, the men heave at the capstans till the boat has passed the equilibrium, when, by its own gravity, it is launched with great velocity into the lower canal, and is prevented from shipping too much water, by a strong skreen of basket-work, which is placed at the head. On the left hand stands a mutilated triumphal arch, and a small temple inclosing an idol, to which sacrifices are frequently made for the preservation of the vessels passing over.

For a plan and section of the above, vide Sir George Staunton's Account, Plate 34 of the folio volume.

London Published Ap'l 1 1798 by G. Nicol Pall mall

PLATE XXX

AN ARROW-MAKER

The staff of the Chinese arrow is, generally, of fir, sometimes of reed, and very neatly made, yet not so highly ornamented as those of the natives of Hindostan. These arrows are armed with a sharp head of iron of a rhombic form, and are thrown with great accuracy from a bow which possesses uncommon missile powers. It is composed of a tough, pliable wood, lined with buffalo horn, and its elasticity is derived from their combined action. The form of this bow, strung, or when the arrow is drawn to the head, exactly resembles that of the ancient Scythians: when unstrung, it flies back, and assumes a figure nearly circular. The bowstring is about the size of a small goose-quill, and is composed of united silken threads.

Pu Quà, Canton, Delin.   Dadley, London, Sou.

Publiſhd May 4 1799 by W. Miller, Old Bond Street, London.

PLATE XXXI

PORTRAIT OF A SOLDIER

in his full Uniform

The empire of China has, since the conquest of the Tartars, enjoyed uninterrupted tranquillity, if we except partial insurrections, &c. and in consequence of this long intermission of service, the Chinese army are become enervated, and want the courage, as well as the discipline, of European troops; for strict order is so little enforced, that it is not uncommon to see many among them fanning themselves while standing in the ranks.

The candidates for promotion, in their army, are required not only to give proofs of their knowledge in military tactics, but they must likewise exhibit trials of personal strength and agility, by shooting at the target, exercising the matchlock, sabre, &c.

The situation of the soldiery is even envied by the lower classes, as they regularly receive their pay, though their services are seldom required, but occasionally to assist in quelling tumults, or doing duty at the military posts; thus, for the greater part of their time, they follow their several occupations, having little else to do than keep their arms and accoutrements bright and in good order, ready for the inspection of the officers, should they be suddenly called out to a review, or any other emergency.

This dress of the troops is clumsy, inconvenient, and inimical to the performance of military exercises, yet a battalion thus equipped has, at some distance, a splendid and even warlike appearance; but on closer inspection these coats of mail are found to be nothing more than quilted nankeen, enriched with thin plates of metal, surrounded with studs, which gives the *tout-ensemble* very much the appearance of armour.

From the crown of the helmet (which is the only part that is iron) issues a spear, inclosed with a tassel of dyed horse-hair. The characters on the breast-plate, denote the corps to which he belongs; and the box which is worn in front, serves to contain heads of arrows, bowstrings, &c. &c. The lower part of the bow is inclosed in a sheath or case.

W. Alexander fecit.

London Publish'd March 1st 1799. by G. Nicol Pallmall.

PLATE XXXII

A PORTER WITH FRUIT-TREES
AND FLOWERS

The Chinese are fond of flowers, and of dwarf fruit-trees, which grow in pots of porcelain, and are placed either upon stands, or the railing of their court-yards: where may be seen not only diminutive orange, peach, and other fruit-trees, but also firs and oaks, stinted in their growth to two feet, by an ingenious, though certainly unnatural contrivance, and exhibiting all the appearances of maturity or decay.

Qua, Canton, Delin.   Dadley, London, Sculp

Published May 1, 1799, by W. Miller, Old Bond Street, London.

PLATE XXXIII

A GROUP OF PEASANTRY, WATERMEN, &c.

playing with Dice

The Chinese are so much addicted to gaming, that they are seldom without a pack of cards, or a set of dice. Cock-fighting is in practice among them; and quails are also bred for the same purpose. They have likewise a large species of grasshopper (or grillæ) common in China; a couple of these are put into a bason to fight, while the by-standers bet sums of money on the issue of the conflict: these insects assail each other with great animosity, frequently tearing off a limb by the violence of their attacks. The Chinese dice are marked exactly similar to those of Europe; in playing they never use a box, but cast them out of the hand. The laws of the empire allowing them full power to dispose of their wives and children, instances have happened when these have been put to the hazard of a throw; and it should be mentioned, that in all their games, whether for amusement or avarice, the Chinese are very noisy and quarrelsome. The figure standing with an instrument of agri-culture in his hand, is an husbandman; another sitting figure, with a small black cap, is a waterman, having by him a gong, which is an instrument of semi-metal resembling a pot-lid; this being struck with the stick lying near it, produces a harsh jarring sound, which is heard at a considerable distance: one of these is always suspended at the head of every vessel when tracked along the canals, and struck as occasion requires, by the people on board, to inform the trackers when to desist hauling, and when to resume their labour. By this method much con-fusion is prevented, where the great concourse of vessels would be con-tinually running foul of each other, if not warned by this contrivance.

These gongs have so many various notes, that the trackers know perfectly when the signal is made from the vessel they are hauling.

W. Alexander fecit.

London Publish'd March 1st 1799. by G. Nicol Pallmall.

PLATE XXXIV

A PEDLAR

The Chinese pedlar carries handkerchiefs, garters, fans, pockets, tobacco-pouches, &c. for sale, upon a bamboo frame of a very simple but well-invented construction. These wares are displayed upon four transverse pieces, which are connected with an upright one. He thus can easily carry the whole upon his shoulder, walk with it as a staff, or present his articles to his customer.

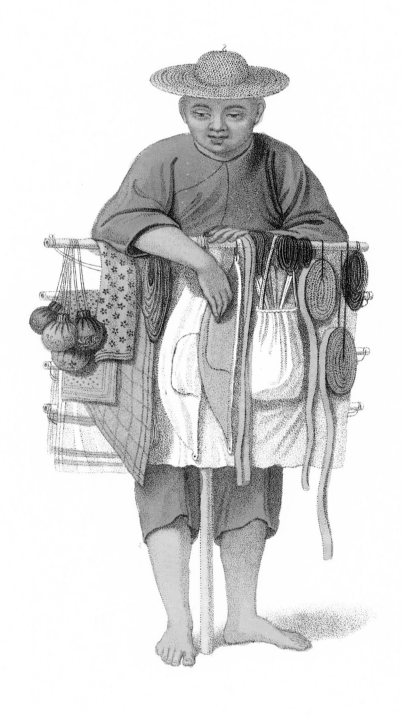

Pu-Qua, Canton, Delin.

Dudley, London, Sculp!

Published May 4,1799, by W. Miller, Old Bond Street, London.

PLATE XXXV

VIEW OF A CASTLE

near the City of Tien-sin

This castle, or tower, is situated on a point of land at the confluence of three rivers, the Pei-ho, the Yun-leang, and the When-ho, near the celestial city (Tien-sin), which is the chief harbour for shipping, and principal depot for merchandize throughout China; and from whence the various articles of commerce are circulated, by means of the canals, through the most distant provinces.

This edifice is thirty-five feet in height, and built with bricks, except the foundation, which is of stone, and has been undermined, most likely by inundation; the surrounding country being very low and marshy. A guard of soldiers is constantly stationed here, and, in cases of tumult or commotion, the centinels give the alarm to the adjacent military posts, in the daytime by hoisting a signal, and at night by the explosion of fire-works; on which the neighbouring garrisons repair to the spot where their services are required.

Within the battlements is a building to shelter centinels on duty; one of them is beating a gong, to announce to the garrison the approach of a viceroy or mandarin of rank; on this notice, they immediately form in a rank, and stand under arms to salute him. Within the parapet a lantern is suspended, and in the opposite angle the imperial standard is elevated; the colour of the tablet, with the inscription on it, likewise shews it to be a royal edifice. In Nieu-hoff's account of the Dutch embassy, which was sent to Pekin in the year 1656, is a print either of this tower, or one similar to it, which stood on the same site. The hillocks of earth under a clump of trees, seen in the distance, are burying-places.

London. Published March 1.st 1799. by G. Nicol. Pallmall.

PLATE XXXVI

A SHOEMAKER

This, like many others of these pictures, is a very accurate portrait of a man who was frequently to be seen in the suburbs of Canton. One basket holds his implements for working; in the other he carries his leather and the stool upon which he occasionally sits. The upper part of a man's shoe in China is commonly made of black cotton cloth, with an edge of white. The sole only is sometimes of leather: this shoe has no straps, and is usually cut square at the toe.

Qua Canton Delin.

Dadley London Sculpt.

Published May 1.1799. by W. Miller, Old Bond Street, London.

PLATE XXXVII

A SEA VESSEL UNDER SAIL

Ships of this construction are employed by the merchants, in conveying the produce of the several provinces to the different ports of the empire.

The hold for the stowage of the various commodities, is divided into several partitions, which are so well caulked, with a composition called chu-nam, as to be water-proof; by this contrivance, in the event of a leak, the greater part of the cargo is preserved from injury, and the danger of foundering considerably removed.

The main and foresails are of matting, strongly interwoven, and extended by spars of bamboo running horizontally across them; the mizen and topsails are nankeen, the latter of which is (contrary to the European method) never hoisted higher than is seen in the drawing. The sails are braced up or eased off, by means of ropes attached to the extremities of the spars in the sails, which are known by the name of a crowfoot; and thus the ship is tacked with very little trouble.

The prow, or head is, as usual with Chinese vessels, without stem; they are likewise without keel, and consequently make considerable leeway. The two anchors are made of a ponderous wood, called by the Chinese tye-mou, or iron wood, the several parts of which are strongly lashed and bolted together, and pointed with iron, though sometimes they carry large grapnels of four shanks. The arched roof of matting is the cabin, in which the seamen sleep, &c. and the bamboo spars on the quarter, are conveniently carried in that situation for the uses of the ship.

The several flags and ensigns, are characteristic of the taste of the Chinese.

London Publish'd March 1:st 1799 by G. Nicol Pallmall.

PLATE XXXVIII

A BLACKSMITH

The basket contains his hammer, pincers, charcoal, &c. together with his bellows, a fuller description of which will be given with a subsequent plate: all these are equipoised by the anvil. Thus, by ingeniously simplifying the implements, which for this occupation are in Europe of the most cumbrous nature, the Chinese blacksmith renders his anvil and forge as portable as a single nail, or a grain of coal-dust.

ua, Canton, Delin.

Dadley. London. Sculp.

Published May 1. 1799. by W. Miller. Old Bond Street. London.

PLATE XXXIX

PORTRAIT OF CHOW-TA-ZHIN

In his Dress of Ceremony

Chow-ta-zhin, a Quan, or Mandarin, holding a civil employment in the state, was, with Van-ta-zhin, entrusted by the Emperor with the care of the British Embassy during its residence in China. He was a man of grave deportment, strict integrity, and sound judgment, as well as of great erudition; having been preceptor to a part of the Imperial family.

His external honours were the customary distinction of a blue ball on his cap; from which was suspended a peacock's feather, being a mark of additional rank.

He is attired in his full court dress, being a loose gown of silk or satin, covering an under vest richly embroidered in silk of the most vivid colours; the square badge on his breast, and its exact counterpart on the back, is also of rich embroidery, and contains the figure of an imaginary bird, which denotes the wearer to be a Mandarin of letters, in like manner as a tiger on the badge would shew the person to be in a military capacity. The beads worn round the neck are occasionally of coral, agate, or of perfumed wood, exquisitely carved, as affluence or fancy may dictate.

In his hand he holds a paper relative to the Embassy.

London Published Dec.r 1.st 1799 by George Nichols Pall mall.

PLATE XL

A LANTERN-PAINTER

The Chinese are very curious in their lanterns. When displayed at their festivals, these are of an extremely large size, of various forms, and very richly ornamented. They are covered with transparent silk or paper whereon are painted flowers, animals, &c. which receive a kind of animation from the light within. That which the figure is employed upon is of the more common sort. Every person who is found in the streets after the watch is set, without a small lantern of this description; bearing his name and place of abode painted upon it, subjects himself to be arrested by the officers of the police.

There is an annual festival called the Feast of Lanterns. It commences on the evening of the thirteenth day of the first month, and continues till the evening of the sixteenth day. On this occasion people in affluent circumstances display lanterns of ten pounds cost: those which are made for viceroys, and other great mandarins, are sometimes valued at one hundred, or one hundred and fifty pounds each.* Their lanterns are rarely if ever made of glass, that composition being very little used in China, unless for mirrors. In their houses the air is generally excluded, and the light admitted by windows made of the semi-transparent shell of the pearl oyster.

* Pausanias the historian relates that the ancient Greeks had also an annual nocturnal illumination, which was styled "Πνρσων Εορτη—The Festival of Torches."

Pa-Qua. Canton. Delin.

Dadley. London. Sculp.

Published, May 4 1799 by W. Miller, Old Bond Street, London.

PLATE XLI

A CHINESE PORTER, OR CARRIER

When the wind is favourable, and where the level face of the country will admit, the Chinese sometimes hoist this simple kind of sail to lessen the exertion of the driver; when the wind is adverse, the sail is laid aside, and another labourer employed to assist in pulling the machine, by means of a rope placed across his shoulders.

The carriage contains, among other articles, some vegetables, a basket of fruit, a box of tea, loose bamboos, and a jar of wine, the stopper of which is covered with clay, to prevent the air injuring the liquor; on the side are placed his hat, and some implements for keeping the machine in order.

This contrivance is thus described by Milton, in his Paradise Lost, Book III. line 437, &c.

> "But in his way lights, on the barren plains
> "Of Sericana, where Chineses drive,
> "With sails and wind, their cany waggons light."

PLATE XLII

A WOMAN PREPARING TEA

Tea (tchà) is always presented to a visitor in China, at whatever time of the day he may arrive. It is served in porcelain cups with covers, and possesses, in its native clime, a peculiarly fine flavour and scent. It is never drank hot, neither does a Chinese ever mix it with cream or sugar.

There is a sort of tea, named Pou-Yùl-Tchà, from its being cultivated near the village of Pou-Yùl, in the province of Yun-Nan. The leaves of this are longer and thicker than of the other sorts, and are rolled up with a viscous liquid into a kind of ball, and dried in the sun. This sort bears a good price amongst the natives; they cut the balls into pieces, and pour the boiling water upon them. This tea is not of a very pleasant taste, but is esteemed very wholesome. Two of its attributed virtues are the curing of the colic, and the creating of an appetite; but perhaps the essential virtues of Tea consist in its being an innocent, refreshing beverage, which quenches thirst; and that, supplying the place of inflammatory liquors, the laborious Chinese porter relishes it equally with the most delicate European lady.

Pu-Qua, Canton, Delin.

Dadley, London, Sculp.ᵗ

Published May 4 1799, by W. Miller, Old Bond Street, London.

PLATE XLIII

THE HABITATION OF A MANDARIN

The house of a Mandarin is generally distinguished by two large poles erected before the gate; in the day-time flags are displayed on these poles as ensigns of his dignity, and during the night painted lanthorns are suspended on them.

The superior Chinese choose to live in great privacy, their habitations therefore are generally surrounded by a wall; their houses seldom exceed one story in height, though there are some few exceptions, as in the residence of the Embassy at Pekin, where one of the many edifices of that palace had apartments above the ground floor, and was occupied by the Secretary of Embassy.

The several rooms of a Chinese house are without ceilings, so that the timbers supporting the roof are exposed. The common articles of furniture are, frames covered with silk of various colours, adorned with moral sentences, written in characters of gold, which are hung in the compartments; on their tables are displayed curious dwarf trees, branches of agate, or gold and silver fish, all which are placed in handsome vessels of porcelain.

London Published Dec.r 17 1796 by G. Nicol, Pall Mall.

PLATE XLIV

A BEGGAR WITH A SERPENT

This miserable medicant carries a live serpent coiled round his neck, the greatest part of which he will, for a very small reward, cram head-foremost into his mouth, allowing any person present to draw it out by the tail.

The Editor of this Work affirms, from his personal knowledge, that this mode of begging, however extraordinary, is practised without the smallest trick or deception.

Pu-Qua, Canton, Delin.

Dadley, London, Sculp.

Published May 1, 1799, by W. Miller, Old Bond Street, London

PLATE XLV

A MANDARIN'S TRAVELLING BOAT

Mandarins, who are employed in travelling from place to place on the public service, keep barges for that purpose, as carriages are kept in England.

They are generally ornamented by painting and varnishing the pannels and mouldings with various devices, &c. At night, or during rain, the part occupied by the Mandarin is inclosed by shutters, and the light is then received through lattices, covered with laminæ of oyster shells.

The gunwale of these barges (as with most Chinese vessels) is sufficiently broad for the watermen, &c. to pass from stem to stern, without inconvenience to passengers in the principal apartments.

The Mandarin is seen attended by soldiers and servants, who are bringing his dinner; the double umbrella, or ensign of his authority, is conspicuously placed to demand respect; the flag and board at the stern, with Chinese characters on them, exhibit his rank and employment; these insignia of power also serve as a signal for other vessels to make clear passage for him, in consequence of which, such boats are seldom obstructed in their progress through the immense number of vessels constantly employed on the canals. The master of any vessel who, by mismanagement, or even accident, should impede these officers in the exercise of their duty, would most likely receive the instant punishment of a certain number of blows from the bamboo, at the discretion of the Mandarin.

London Published Dec 31st 1799 by G. Nicol, Pallmall.

PLATE XLVI

A TRAVELLER

This is designed to represent a poor person, perhaps a pilgrim, travelling on foot, and oppressed with excessive grief or weariness. His dress indicates that he is in mourning. He carries a staff, a species of bramble which grows in some parts of China, and is frequently made use of as a walking-stick. The idea may be indulged, that this is a person either proceeding to or returning from visiting the tomb of a departed relative; it being a rule with the Chinese to extend their sentiments and duty of filial pity even to "that country from whose bourne no traveller returns." The names of the deceased are inscribed upon a tablet, and placed in a large room in their house, called the "Hall of Ancestors," and to which, at stated periods, the surviving kindred do homage; observing likewise an annual custom of repairing to the cemeteries of their forefathers; where, mindful of the honoured dead, they renew their lamentations over the sacred dust, and arrest the ravages of time in his attacks, whether upon the high trophied tomb, or humble mouldering heap.

Pu Qua, Canton, Delin.

Dadley, London, Sculp.

Published May 4, 1799, by W. Miller, Old Bond Street, London.

PLATE XLVII

A STANDARD BEARER

Early in the morning of the 30th of September, 1793, the Embassador and suite proceeded on their journey northward, to pay the customary compliment of meeting the Emperor, who was then returning from his summer residence in Tartary, to his palace at Pekin; on this occasion, each side of the road was lined, as far as the eye could reach, with mandarines, soldiers, &c. bearing banners, large silk triple umbrellas, and other insignia of Chinese royalty. The Print represents a soldier employed in bearing a standard, or gilt board, on which are depicted characters, which probably display some title of the Emperor.

His dress is nankeen cotton, which is tied round the waist, with the imperial or yellow girdle, and his legs are cross-gartered: his hat is straw, neatly woven, and fastened under the chin; the crown is covered with a fringe of red silk, converging from the centre, where a feather is placed.

His sword, as is customary with the Chinese, is worn with the hilt behind.

W. Alexander fec.

London Published Oct.r 19. 1800, by G. & W. Nicol Pallmall.

PLATE XLVIII

A DISTILLER

The liquor drunk by the higher classes of people in China is a sort of wine extracted from rice, which is steeped for some days in water, together with other ingredients; they afterwards boil it, and during the fermentation it throws up a vaporous scum. A pure liquor, in taste and strength very much resembling inferior Rhenish, is found under this scum, which is drawn off into jars. Of the lees a kind of spirit is made, which is very potent and fiery.—It is a custom with Chinese to drink all their wine very hot.

Pu-Qua, Canton, Delin.

Dadley, London, Sculp.

Published May 4, 1799, by W. Miller, Old Bond Street, London.

PLATE XLIX

A SACRIFICE AT THE TEMPLE

The Chinese have no regular sabbath, or fixed time for worshipping the Deity in congregation. Their temples being constantly open, are visited by the supplicants on every important undertaking, such as an intended marriage, the commencement of a long journey, building a house, &c.

The figure on the right hand is anxiously watching the fall of tallies, which he is shaking in a joint of bamboo; these are severally marked with certain characters, and as they fall, the characters are inserted by the priest in the book of fate. After the ceremony, the priest communicates to the votary the success of his prayers, which has been thus determined by lot.

The priesthood always shave the head entirely, and wear a loose dress of silk or nankeen, the colour of which is characteristic of their particular sect.

The figure kneeling before the sacred urn, in which perfumed matches are burning, is about to perform a sacrifice. On these occasions round pieces of gilt and silvered paper are burnt in tripods for that purpose, and at the same time quantities of crackers are discharged.

Behind the figures are seen two hideous idols. These statues are usually arranged against the walls of the temple, inclosed within a railing.

W. Alexander

London, Publish'd Oct 19 1800, by G & W. Nicol. Pallmall.

PLATE L

A FISHERMAN

He uses the machine which he carries upon his shoulder to catch fish. It consists of several pieces of blue calico, distended by transverse slips of rattan, fixed to small poles, and connected together by strings. This is opened in the manner of a folding screen, and the poles being planted in the bottom of standing water, it obstructs the passage of the fish.

The Chinese have various methods of catching fish. Some travellers describe a particular sort of bird, a kind of pelican, which is trained for that purpose.

Pu-Quà, Canton, Delin.

Dadley, London, Sculp.

Publish'd May 4 1799, by W. Miller, Old Bond Street, London.

PLATE LI

A MILITARY STATION

Along the canals and public roads of China, great numbers of military posts are erected, at which eight or ten soldiers are generally stationed.

Adjacent to each of these stands a look-out-house, commanding an extensive prospect; and adjoining are placed five cones of plastered brick work, out of which certain combustibles are said to be fired, in times of alarm from invasion or insurrection. In front of the building is a simple triumphal entrance, on which is an inscription suitable to the place. Near this the imperial ensign is elevated; and on the left of the house is a frame of wood, in which are deposited different arms, as pikes, matchlocks, bows, &c.

The vessel passing by with a double umbrella, contains some mandarin of distinction, who is saluted by the firing of three petards,* and by the guard, who are drawn out in a rank.

* The Chinese, on these occasions, never use more than three guns, which are always fired perpendicularly, to prevent accidents.

Willm Alexander fec.^t

London Publish'd Octr 19. 1800. by G & W. Nicol. Pallmall.

PLATE LII

AN APOTHECARY

Itinerant apothecaries, and venders of drugs, are very numerous in China, who are occasionally either surgeons or physicians, and whose ignorance of prime causes is attended with the same mischievous effects as that of similar practitioners in Europe. The Chinese pretend to discover every disorder by the beat of the pulse, which their physicians feel in various parts of the body. They have much faith in the use of simples, which they recommend as specifics in most disorders. Their druggists have great shops furnished with medicines, and there are fairs where nothing but simples and remedies are sold.—In China every body is allowed to practise physic: this privilege, whether granted or connived at by the government, multiplies quacks, of whom the vulgar entertain a very high opinion, and suffer accordingly. It is related, that great sagacity is displayed by the Chinese in discovering whether a person has died a natural death, or in consequence of some violence, and this even after the body has begun to corrupt. The corpse is taken out of the grave, and washed in vinegar. After this, a large fire is kindled in a pit dug on purpose, six feet long, three wide, and the same in depth; this fire is continually augmented, until the surrounding earth becomes as hot as an oven. The remaining fire is taken from the pit, a large quantity of their wine is poured into it, and it is covered with a hurdle made of osier twigs, upon which the body is stretched out at full length. A cloth is thrown over all, in the form of an arch, in order that the steam may act upon it in every direction. At the expiration of two hours this cloth is taken off; and it is asserted, that if any blows have been given, they will appear upon the body, in whatever state it may be. The same experiment is extended even to bones stripped of their flesh; the Chinese assuring us, that if the blows have been so servere as to occasion death, this process causes the marks to appear upon the bones, although none of them may be broken, or visibly injured.

..., Canton, Delin.   _Dadley. London. Sculp._

Publish'd May 4, 1799, by W. Miller, Old Bond Street, London.

PLATE LIII

A FISHING BOAT

This Print illustrates a contrivance of the Chinese fishermen for raising their nets: the frame work is composed of that most useful plant the bamboo, which, uniting strength with lightness, is made use of on almost every occasion. When the weight of a man at the extremity of the lever is insufficient to lift a large draught of fish, he is assisted by a companion, as in the representation; the rest of the company are employed at dinner, steering, &c. protected from the sun and weather by a rude covering of mats: the boat is also provided with grapnels, and a lantern to prevent accidents at night. The distance is a view of the lake Poo-yang. On the left hand, near the benches, are some mounds of earth, which occur occasionally for several miles together; the purpose generally assigned to them is the repairing any accidental breach of the canal, with all possible expedition.

Another mode of fishing, often practised by the Chinese, is by means of a species of pelican, called the Leu-tze. See the Account of the British Embassy, by Sir George Staunton, Vol. II. p. 388.

W. Alexander

London Published Oct 19 1800 by G & W Nicol Pall mall.

PLATE LIV

A LABOURER

This shows a kind of wheel-barrow used by the labourers in China for heavy articles, which are thus tied upon it; being of a considerably lighter construction than those in England.

They have also another barrow which is peculiar to the country. It is very large, and requires two men to conduct it, one being placed in front to draw and assist the propelling force. When the wind blows briskly from a contrary direction to the point the labourer is going, he places a square mat stretched between two upright poles, which are fastened on each side of the barrow. This land-sail renders the assistance of the man in front unnecessary, neither has the one in the rear any trouble but to keep the machine steady, and right before the wind.

In this plate is shown the method of carrying the large hat when the head is weary of it.

Qua, Canton Delin.

Dadley, London, Sculp.

Publish'd May 4, 1799, by W. Miller, Old Bond Street, London.

PLATE LV

A CHINESE COMEDIAN

Theatrical exhibitions form one of the chief amusements of the Chinese; for though no public theatre is licensed by the government, yet every Mandarin of rank has a stage erected in his house, for the performance of dramas, and his visitors are generally entertained by actors hired for the purpose.

On occasions of public rejoicing, as the commencement of a new year, the birth-day of the Emperor, and other festivals, plays are openly performed in the streets, throughout the day, and the strolling players rewarded by the voluntary contributions of the spectators.

While the Embassador and his suite were at Canton, theatrical representations were regularly exhibited at dinner time, for their diversion. This character, which the Interpreter explained to be an enraged military officer, was sketched from an actor performing his part before the embassy, December 19, 1793.

These entertainments are accompanied by music: during the performance of which, sudden bursts, from the harshest wind instruments, and the sonorous gong, frequently stun the ears of the audience.

Females are not allowed to perform: their characters are therefore sustained by eunuchs; who, having their feet closely bandaged, are not easily distinguished from women.

The dresses worn by players, are those of ancient times.

W. Alexander fect.

London Published Augt 13th 1801, by G and W. Nicol Pallmall.

PLATE LVI

A MENDER OF PORCELAIN

This ware is so common in China, that most of the ordinary utensils of the house are made of it; dishes, cups, jars, basons, flower-pots; in short, whatsoever serves for ornament or use.

Porcelain consists, principally, of two kinds of native earth, the pètun-tsè and the kao-lìn; these are reduced by water and pounding to a doughy consistency, after having been carefully freed from all impurities by repeated skimming and pouring off. The mass is then kneaded by treading, in order to prepare it for the wheel or mould, from whence, having received its form, it is taken and polished. Porcelain is varnished and baked in an oven; then being painted and gilded, it is baked a second time. The utmost attention is required in the baking, and it is not easy to regulate the proper degree of heat, since any alteration in the weather having an immediate effect on the fire, fuel, and porcelain itself, influences the process.

This old man is working with a small drill pointed by a diamond; through the holes he introduces a very fine wire, and thus renders the bason again fit for service.

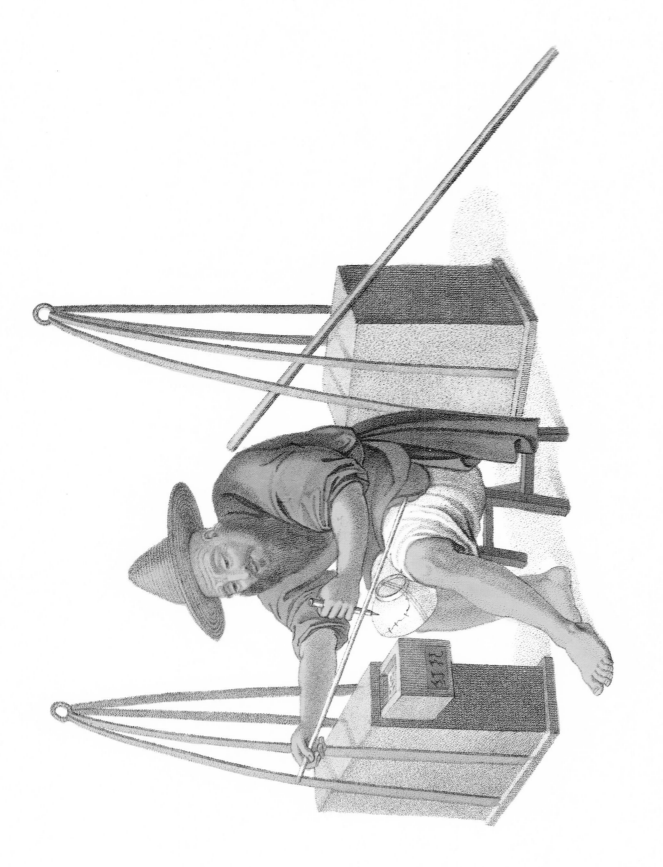

Published . May 4 1799. by W. Miller, Old Bond Street London.

Pu Qnu Canton Foliu

Pullis London Sculp.

PLATE LVII

A GROUP OF CHINESE

Habited for Rainy Weather

During the rainy seasons, the natives of China wear an external dress, well calculated to keep them dry, and prevent, in a great measure, such diseases as arise from exposure to wet.

Watermen, peasantry, and others, employed in the open air, are generally provided with a coat made of straw, from which the rain runs off, as from the feathers of an aquatic bird: in addition to this, they sometimes wear a cloak, formed of the stalks of kow-liang (millet), which completely covers the shoulders; and a broad hat, composed of straw and split bamboo, which defends them both from sun and rain. A Chinese thus equipped (as is the standing figure,) may certainly defy the heaviest showers.

The soldier, under an umbrella of oiled canvas, wears his undress; consisting of a jacket, of black nankeen, bordered with red; behind him is his child, to whom he is likewise affording shelter.

The figure smoking, is habited in a large coat, of skin, with the hair, or wool, remaining on it: sometimes the coat is turned, and the hairy side worn inwards.

Alexander fecit

London Published Aug.ᵗ 13. 1801. by G. and W. Nicol Pallmall.

PLATE LVIII

A BRICKLAYER

The trowel and line, and the method of laying the bricks, resemble those used in Europe. The Chinese houses are, for the most part, on a ground floor, those of the merchants excepted, who have warehouses and workrooms on another story; withinside they are neatly ornamented with varnishing and gilding, but have very little furniture. Their bricks are long, wide, and thin, and they are generally, from the mode of burning, of a greyish blue colour. The streak of mortar is exceedingly minute, appearing at a small distance to be only a narrow line marked with white chalk. Foundations of stone are laid for buildings of size and consequence.

Pe-Qua, Canton, Delin.

Dadley, London, Sculp.

Published May 4 1799, by W. Miller, Old Bond Street, London.

PLATE LIX

A PAGODA OR TEMPLE

For religious Worship

The Chinese are scrupulously observant of moral and religious duties; and their country abounds with temples, of various forms, to which they resort, on every interesting occasion, and offer their sacrifices. Besides these temples, a small tabernacle, or niche, containing their household gods, is to be found in almost every house and ship.

Some religious ceremonies of the Chinese resemble those of the Church of Rome: and the Chinese Idol, denominated Shin-moo, is very similar to the representations of the Virgin and Child; both being figures of a female and an infant, with rays of glory issuing from their heads and having lights burning before them, during the day as well as night.

The greater part of the people, are of the sect of Fo; whose followers believe in the metempsychosis, and in a future state of happiness, after a virtuous life; and suppose, that the souls of the irreligious live hereafter in a state of suffering, and subject to the hardships endured by inferior animals.

The figures dressed in loose gowns, are priests, attending at the temple; and the background, is a view of the city Tin-hai, Nov. 21, 1793.

London Published Aug.ᵗ 13.1801. by G. and W. Nicol, Pallmall.

PLATE LX

A CARPENTER

This itinerant handicraftsman carries all his tools, his saw excepted, in a box upon his shoulder. His staff serves him for a rule, and the box is used alternately as a seat or bench to work upon.

Qua, Canton, Delin.

Dadley, London, Sculp.

Publish'd May 4.1799. by W. Miller, Old Bond Street, London.

PLATE LXI

A SHIP OF WAR

The Chinese are so well supplied with the produce of their own country, as to require very little from distant lands; and it is to this native abundance the low state of navigation among them ought to be attributed.

Though they are said to have been acquainted with the use of the compass, from the earliest ages, yet they cannot be considered as expert seamen, either in their application of astronomy to nautical purposes, or skill in manœuvring their clumsy ships.

The compass is, however, an instrument venerated by the seamen, as a deity; and to which they sometimes offer sacrifices of flesh and fruit.

The drawing was made from a ship (Pin-gee-na) lying at anchor in the river, near Ning-po. These vessels may properly be termed floating garrisons; as they contain many soldiers, and are generally stationed near their principal towns.

These soldiers often hang their shields against the ship's quarter; and the rudder is lifted, by ropes, nearly out of the water, perhaps to preserve it, while at anchor.

The ports are false; as few ships of the Chinese navy are, at present, supplied with artillery.

W. Alexander fec.^t

London Published Augt 13.th 1801. by G. and W. Nicol Pallmall.

PLATE LXII

A MANDARIN IN HIS SUMMER DRESS

This long, loose habit is admirably well adapted to warm weather; and to every article of wearing apparel the Chinese have shewn a wise attention. Their shirts are of different kinds of cloth, according to the season. In summer many wear a silken net upon their skin, which, interposing betwixt that and the next garment, relieves them from the inconvenience of copious perspiration. Their shoes, during that season, are neatly and airily composed of weaved rattan. They wear likewise a light cap of the same material, ornamented with red hair, and they usually carry a handkerchief and a fan; the latter being not only a useful, but also a formal article of dress with a Chinese in warm weather, and is carried even by their military during the summer. Their idea of perfect beauty in a man is, a large forehead, a short nose, small well-cut eyes, a large and square face, the ears broad, a middling-sized mouth, and black hair. They think a man well made when he is large and fat, and fills a chair with a good grace. The excessive heats of the southern provinces give to their peasants and mechanics a brown complexion, yet the generality of Chinese are not naturally dark. It is usual for their literati, and their men of wealth, to wear the nails of their fingers upwards of two inches in length, in order to demonstrate that they do not earn their livelihood by manual occupations.

The Chinese of real rank, civil or military, the latter emanating from the former, entertain the most contemptuous sentiments of those whose lives are occupied in the concerns of commerce. They consider common honesty in a trader as the offspring of design. They affect to despise equally the importance of the merchant, and the meanness and sordid practices of the overreacher, suspecting that the insatiable and immoral passion of avarice holds the same degree of influence over the minds of both: that the soul once subjected to its dominion, sinks, and becomes paralysed to every action of generosity, elegance, or true greatness; and that the *auri sacra fames* instigates those unhappily possessed by it to consider no means unsanctioned, no sacrifices too considerable, which may lead to the completion of its selfish desires.—The Emperor of China assigns the second rank in society to those whose occupation is the tillage of the earth, and, attended by the princes of his court, annually guides, with his own hand, a plough through a plot of ground selected for that purpose.—The third and last class is composed of mechanics, merchants, and others.

The meritorious actions of mandarins in power are entered in a public register, which is styled "The Book of Merit;" and with these honourable records are joined their respective titles. Although there is no Book of Infamy, yet if those personages behave ill, they are punished by his Imperial Majesty without much hesitation; they are deprived of their titles, and a kind of nick-name is attached to their surname, expressive of the cause of their disgrace.

... Canton, Delin.   Dadley, London, Sculp.

Publish'd May 4. 1799, by W. Miller, Old Bond Street, London.

PLATE LXIII

A SOLDIER IN HIS COMMON DRESS

The army of China cannot be considered formidable, their troops being naturally effeminate, and without the courage of European soldiers: one reason assigned for this is a mode of education which is not calculated to inspire a nation with courage, and it may partly be accounted for, from their having enjoyed uninterrupted peace since their subjugation by the Tartars.

Every soldier, on his marriage, and on the birth of a male child, is intitled to a donation from the Emperor; and the family of a deceased soldier receives likewise a gift of condolence.

The undress of a Chinese or Tartar soldier consists of a short jacket of black or red nankeen, with a border of another colour; under this is a garment of the same material, with long sleeves: when the weather is cold, one or more dresses are worn under this. The flag at his back is of silk, and fastened by means of a socket attached behind: these are generally worn by every fifth man, and make a very gay appearance.

Their bows are of elastic wood, covered on the outside with a layer of horn, and require the power of from seventy to one hundred pounds in drawing them; the string is composed of silk threads closely woulded, and the arrows are well made and pointed with steel. Their scymeters, though rudely formed, are said to equal the best from Spain.

The military establishment of China, including cavalry and infantry, consists of 1,800,000 men. Vide the Appendix to Sir G. Staunton's Account of the Embassy to China.

London Published Dec.r 1 1800 by W. Miller Old Bond Street

PLATE LXIV

A STONE-HEWER

In general, the stone which is hewn for the edifices in China, is cut remarkably thin in proportion to its length, being perhaps only half a foot in thickness, though it be two or three feet in width, and six in length. Many of the smaller bridges are made of such stones, laid like planks, on piers. This figure is working with a pointed chisel, and a little iron-headed mallet. His screen prevents the chippings from giving annoyance to any one passing by him.

Pu-Quà, Cantòn, Delin.

Dadley, London, Sculpt.

Published May 4, 1799, by W. Miller Old Bond Street London.

PLATE LXV

THE PUNISHMENT OF THE BASTINADO

Is frequently used in China, for slight offences, and occasionally inflicted on all ranks.

When the number of blows sentenced by the Mandarin are few, it is considered as a gentle chastisement or fatherly correction, and when given in this mild way is not disgraceful, though the culprit is obliged, on his knees, with his forehead touching the ground, to thank the magistrate who so kindly ordered it to be administered.

Every Mandarin whose degree of nobility does not exceed the blue ball on his cap, is subject to this castigation, when ordered by his superior; but all above that rank can only be bastinadoed at the command of the Emperor.

The instrument used on these occasions is a split bamboo, several feet long, which is applied on the posteriors, and, in crimes of magnitude, with much severity. In petty offences, the offender (if he has the means) contrives dexterously to bribe the executioner, who, in proportion to the extent of the reward, mitigates the violence of the punishment, by laying the strokes on lightly, though with a feigned strength, to deceive the Mandarin; and it is said, that, for a douceur, some are ready to receive the punishment intended for the culprit; though, when eighty or a hundred blows is the sentence, it sometimes affects the life of the wretched criminal.

When a Mandarin is from home, he is generally attended by an officer of police, and perhaps one or more soldiers, who are ordered in this summary way to administer some half dozen blows on any careless person who might negligently omit the customary salute of dismounting his horse, or kneeling in the road before the great man as he passes by.

London Published Jan.ᵗʰ 1ˢᵗ 1822 by J. and W. Nicol, Pall Mall

PLATE LXVI

A PILLOW SELLER

The common classes of Chinese sleep upon a boarded bedstead, whereon is placed a kind of rug. Their covering at night consists of part of the dress they wear by day; this they throw aside or retain, according to the temperature of the atmosphere, which frequently varies, in a few hours, an astonishing number of degrees.* The Chinese use cane pillows, particularly in summer, or when travelling, which they sometimes cover with leather or skins. They are very light and elastic. Some of these pillows, being hollow, are converted into a kind of trunk or portmanteau, and serve as a receptacle for writings, &c.

* Five and forty degrees in the space of twenty-four hours.

Pu-Quà, Canton, Delin.

Dadley, London, Sculp.

Published May 4, 1799, by W. Miller, Old Bond Street, London.

PLATE LXVII

A PAI-LOU, OR TRIUMPHAL ARCH

These monuments are erected for the purpose of transmitting the meritorious actions of good men to posterity. Magistrates who have executed the duties of their high office with justice and integrity; heroes who have signalized themselves in the field; and others of meaner station whose virtues or superior learning intitle them thereto, often receive this high honour, which likewise serves the purpose of exciting their posterity to the same virtuous actions.

These Pai-lous (usually translated, triumphal arches) are built at the public expense, generally with stone, though sometimes the better sort are made of marble, and some inferior ones of wood; the chief of them have four uprights, each of one stone, which is often thirty feet in length; horizontally across these are placed the transoms or friezes, on which the inscription is engraved with letters of gold, &c. and the summit of the fabric is crowned with projecting roofs richly ornamented.

This was drawn from one near the city of Ning-po, Nov. 17, 1793, where many others are erected, some of which were of a meaner kind, and had but two uprights. The inscription on this was thus translated by a Chinese attendant on the Embassy: "By the Emperor's supreme goodness, in the 59th year of Tchien-Lung, and on the first day, this triumphal edifice was erected in honour of Tchoung-ga-chung, the most high and learned Doctor of the Empire, and one of the Mandarins of the Tribunal of Arms."

PLATE LXVIII

A FLUTE SELLER

The flutes used in China are about two feet and a half in length, and have twelve holes. They are made of a species of bamboo, and produce a soft pleasing sound. The Chinese, in general, learn all their tunes by ear; but it is said that of late years some few among them have acquired the European method of marking down musical notes. There is great monotony, and want of expression in the sounds of Chinese musical instruments; the loud crash, proceeding from the united powers of gongs, cymbals, drums, &c. which is introduced at intervals, excepted. A band of musicians always performs at the representation of their plays, and other entertainments: in a theatre they are posted, in full view, at the back part of the stage—a disposition which is far from adding to the interest of the scene, or increasing the stage-effect.

Pu-Quà, Canton, Delin.

Dadley, London, Sculp.t

Publish'd May 4 1799, by W. Miller, Old Bond Street, London.

PLATE LXIX

VESSELS PASSING THROUGH
A SLUICE

The imperial, or grand canal of China, extends, with little interruption, from Canton, in lat. about 23° 15′, to Pekin in 30° 50′.

From this main trunk issue many branches, which pass through
innumerable cities, towns, and villages, as roads through European
countries; and by this means a communication is kept up with the utmost
limits of the Empire; some lesser canals are also cut to counteract the
overwhelming effects of inundation; these at the same time serve to
convey superfluous water over the low lands for the nutriment of rice,
which requires immersion in water till it approaches maturity.

Locks and sluices of various kinds are therefore very numerous; the
Print exhibits one chiefly designed as a bridge for the accommodation of
foot passengers; the building on the right hand serves to shelter those
who are employed in raising the bridge, as well as to preserve the stone
under it, which records the name, &c. of the individual who was at the
expense of its erection.

Some sluices are so constructed as to retain a considerable body of
water for the use of vessels of greater draught; these have grooves cut
in the masonry at the opposite piers, into which strong and heavy boards
are dropped, similar to a portcullis, and when a sufficient quantity of
water is collected, the planks are drawn up and the vessels pass through
with considerable velocity, having previously paid a small toll for their
admission through the sluice.

The vessel having the yellow or royal flag, is one inhabited by a part
of the Embassy; some others occupied by the English have already passed
through.

PLATE LXX

A BALANCER

The Asiatics are all remarkably expert at manual feats; but no people seem to have brought the art of balancing to such a degree of perfection as the Chinese.

The man represented in this Plate gives to a porcelain jar an appearance of locomotive power: by an imperceptible action of the muscles, it is made, without any other impelling force, to glide along his arms, while they are extended in an horizontal position; he then, balancing himself upon one foot, poises the jar upon his knuckles, where it remains fixed without motion.

Pu-Quà, Cantòn, Delin.

Dadley, London, Sculp.

Publish'd May 4 1799, by W. Miller, Old Bond Street, London.

PLATE LXXI

A MANDARIN

attended by a Domestic

Though chairs are commonly used in China, yet the Chinese sometimes choose to sit in the manner of the Turks.

This Mandarin, habited in his court attire, is one of the literati, and a civil magistrate, which is known by the bird embroidered in the badge on his breast: his high rank and honour are likewise denoted by the red ball and peacock's feather with three eyes attached to his cap, as also by the beads of pearl and coral appending from his neck; he is sitting in form on a cushion, smoking, and waiting the arrival of a visitor.

The servant bears in his hand a purse containing tobacco for his master; his girdle encloses a handkerchief, and from which also hangs his tobacco pouch and pipe. On the walls of the apartment Chinese characters are painted, signifying moral precepts.

W. Alexander fecit

London Published Oct.r 1.st 1803 by W. Miller Old Bond Street.

PLATE LXXII

A MAN STRIKING A SMALL GONG DURING AN ECLIPSE

The gong, or loo, is a loud-sounding instrument peculiar to the Chinese. It is a plate of composite metal made of tin, zinc, and copper, with a narrow rim. The larger gongs, in which there is said to be a small quantity of silver, are used in concerts, in military bands, and not unfrequently as bells; they are struck with a great wooden mallet, and may be heard at the distance of several miles. The sound is very solemn, resembling a bell, but shriller or deeper, according to the force with which they are beaten.

This figure represents the performance of a solemn rite, of most antique origin, but punctually observed by the Chinese at this present hour.*

The government of China, which endeavours to render itself the fountain of science and wisdom as it is of power, retains all the skilful astronomers in the capital of Pekin. These, from their knowledge of the celestial bodies, predict eclipses with much accuracy, and communicate their observations to the Emperor. Some months before an eclipse is to appear, the Grand Coláo, or prime-minister, announces it by proclamation, and myriads of people in the most distant provinces are prepared to perform the ceremonies enjoined on the occasion: these chiefly consist in kneeling down, and striking the ground with their foreheads, accompanied by an hideous noise of drums, trumpets, and *gongs*, which are unremittingly persevered in until the eclipse is over. The Chinese consider a frightful din to be a grand specific against malignant spirits; and the notions of an eclipse among the lower ranks of people are, either that God (for they have some idea of a Supreme Being) is very much displeased, or that the luminary is in danger of being destroyed by an aerial monster.†

---

* On the 17th of November, 1789, the Editor of this work was gratified with the opportunity of contemplating, from amidst the shipping at Whampóa, the gloomy grandeur of a total eclipse of the sun at ten o'clock in the forenoon. A few of the larger stars were visible for the space of three minutes; and during the whole time of the eclipse, the surrounding scene, enveloped in imperfect darkness, was most singularly picturesque. The Chinese, regarding a solar eclipse to be replete with dire portent, either awaited the conclusion with timid stillness, or shook the air with unavailing noises; whilst the Europeans, more enlightened, beheld the phenomenon with reverential curiosity, and being supported by that superior knowledge, which enabled them to "look through Nature, up to Nature's GOD," regarded his influence over the planets, and confided in his attributes for restoring that order of which they knew him to be the essence.

† Tibullus, Ovid, Livy, Juvenal, Tacitus, and other writers, have noticed the practice among the ancients of striking upon sonorous instruments, to relieve or rescue a celestial luminary from, what they also imagined to be, the preternatural or evil influence of an eclipse.

Pu Quà, Canton, Delin.

Dadley, London, Sculp.ᵗ

Published May 4, 1799, by W. Miller, Old Bond Street, London.

PLATE LXXIII

A SMALL IDOL TEMPLE

commonly called a Joss House

The general religion of China, Paganism, generates the grossest superstition and credulity among the unenlightended part of the people, who attribute every casual occurrence to the influence of some good or ill star; if the event forebode evil, they immediately repair to the proper idol with offerings, that the impending misfortune may be averted; if good, they also make sacrifices and return thanks.

These sacred edifices are commonly situated near the road side, or on the banks of canals for the convenience of travellers, &c. who are often observed prostrating before them; some are erected at the public expence, and dedicated to former Emperors, Mandarins, and others, for services rendered to their country; and some are built by charitable persons, to extend religious worship among the people.

On days of general rejoicing, as the commencement of the new year, new moon, Emperor ploughing the ground, feast of lanterns, &c. these buildings are much frequented, the people offering before the little gilt images inhabiting the fabric sacrifices of ready dressed animal food, fish, rice, and wine, in proportion to their ability or inclination; while innumerable crackers are fired, and a profusion of gilt paper and incense is burnt before the idol.

Sometimes a priest attends on such occasions to receive these offerings for the benefit of his fraternity, though more frequently the sacrifices of each suppliant are taken to his family and eaten as a feast. The buildings in the back ground are the residence of a Mandarin, known by the two flag staffs at the entrance: on the hill is a military station and a mutilated Pagoda, these being generally erected on an eminence.

W Alexander feet.

London Published Oct.r 1.st 1803 by W.m Miller Old Bond Street.

PLATE LXXIV

A TINKER

The Chinese has, as was observed in the description of Plate XXXVIII. great advantages in his portable forge, by affording him the means of mending, and even of making upon the spot, iron articles for ordinary use. The solder is melted in the small crucibles which are seen near this figure; it is then applied in its fused state to the breaches of the iron pan, which it effectually repairs, and renders the utensil as service-able as ever.

The original invention of bellows is perhaps unknown, but may be presumed to have existed almost from the discovery of fire—certainly ever since metallurgy was first practised. Strabo* attributes the first discovery of bellows to the philosopher and traveller Anacharsis.

The Chinese bellows differ from those of any other country, and are the best, although the simplest, contrivance of the kind. They consist of a wooden cylinder, with a piston of iron exactly fitted, and having an opening at the side through which the air is forced by the action of the piston, as it is made to approach either end of the cylinder. This plate shews the facility with which these bellows are worked. They are placed with one end upon the ground, the other a little elevated, and are steadied by a large stone upon the top. The piston-rod has a small transverse handle; and in this manner the Chinese effects, with a slight alternate motion of his elbow, what requires an exertion of almost all the muscles in the body of an European. The whole forge is also comprised in a three-legged iron vessel, containing charcoal, and receiving the blast of air ejected from the cylinder as described.

* Strabo, edit. Paris. ann. 1620, lib. vii. page 303.—Τον Ανάχαρτιν ὰ θρωπον σορὸν χαλῶν ὁ Εφοροζ—ινρημτά τε αὐτοµ λεγων τά ζώπνρα.

Pu Qua, Canton, Delin.

Dadley, London, Sculp.

Publish'd May 1, 1799, by W. Miller, Old Bond Street, London.

PLATE LXXV

CHINESE GAMBLERS

with Fighting Quails

It is more common in China to breed quails for fighting, than to bring up game-cocks, for the same purpose, in Europe. The male quails, descended from a good stock, are trained with great care; their owners teaching them to fight most furiously, and with a spirit equalling the best of our game-cocks. These battles, though forbidden by the laws, are countenanced and even practised by the Mandarins; and it is a favourite diversion among the eunuchs in attendance at the palace, who often hazard large sums in bets on the issue of a contest. If during a conflict between these little furies, both birds should happen to fall together, that which last endeavours to peck at his adversary, is deemed the victor.

It is said, that oftentimes on the result of these battles, not only the fortune, but even the wives and children of the parties wagering, are put to the chance of being given up to the winner as concubines and servants.

The figure smoking, holds in his hand some Chinese money threaded on a string; the man with a feather behind his cap is betting with him.

London, Published Sep.r 1.st 1803 by W. Miller Old Bond Street.

PLATE LXXVI

A PUPPET-SHOW

A person mounted on a stool, and concealed as far as the ankles with a covering of blue calico, causes some very small puppets to perform a kind of play, the box at the top representing a stage. The little figures are made to move with much grace and decorum, on which account the Chinese puppet-show is rendered equally innocent as trifling, and may be presented without endangering the purity of the infant mind.

The Chinese youth receive the earliest impressions of virtue and filial obedience; these precepts prevent their incurring the penalties prescribed in the code of laws of that empire against such "degenerate vipers"* as shall dare to violate any of those sacred ties which GOD and Nature have framed to attach them to the authors of their existence. The son, or grandson, of a Chinese, who is deficient in his duty towards his father or mother, grandfather, or grandmother, is condemned by the law to receive one hundred blows of a bamboo; if he gives them abusive language, he is strangled; if he lifts his hand against them, he is beheaded; and if he wounds or maims them, his flesh is torn from his bones with red-hot pincers, and he is cut into a thousand pieces. It is also conjectured that the stability and uniformity of the Chinese character—immutable for the known duration of four thousand years—it is supported solely by that progressive submission which rises, gradually, from the bosom of a family even to the throne.

* See Shakespeare's Lear.

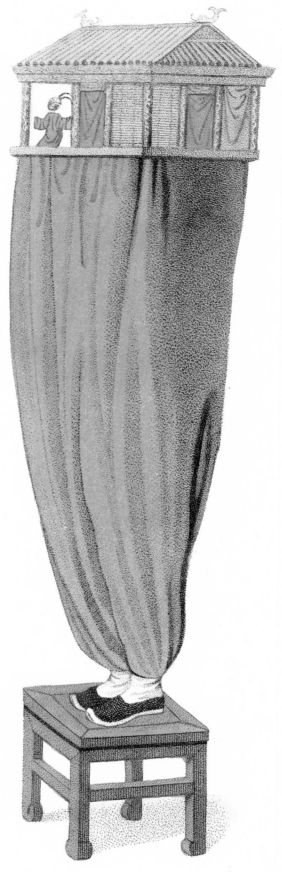

Pu-Quà, Cantòn, Delin.

Dadley, London, Sculp!

Publish'd May 4, 1799, by W. Miller, Old Bond Street, London.

PLATE LXXVII

PORTRAITS OF SEA VESSELS

generally called Junks

On the 5th of August, 1793, the Embassador and his suite left the Lion and Hindostan, and embarked on board the brigs Clarence, Jackall, and Endeavour, when they immediately sailed for the Pay-ho, or White River, in the Gulph of Pe-tchi-li: the other persons attached to the Embassy followed in Junks engaged for that purpose. These vessels, which also conveyed the presents for the Emperor, baggage, &c. are clumsily constructed, and carry about two hundred tons; nevertheless, being flat-bottomed, they draw but little water, and are thereby enabled to cross the shallows at the entrances of the Chinese rivers.

These Junks are of the same form at stem and stern, and the hold is divided into compartments, each being water-tight: the masts are of one tree, and very large; their main and fore sails are of matting, composed of split bamboos and reeds interwoven together; the mizen sails are of nankeen cloth.

The rudders, (which are generally lifted out of the water when at anchor,) are rudely formed, and cannot be worked with dexterity; the steering compasses are placed near them, and surrounded with perfumed matches.

The anchor of four points is of iron, the other of wood; at the quarters are stowed some bamboo spars; and these junks are gaudily adorned with ensigns, vanes, &c. agreeably to the Chinese taste.

W. Alexander fecit.

London Published Sepr 1st 1803 by W. Miller, Old Bond Street.

PLATE LXXVIII

A FISHMONGER

China is a country well stored with fish; even the ditches are stocked with them, which yield a great profit. One of the best sorts resembles the sea-bream; it is commonly sold for little more than one farthing a pound, and generally weighs five or six. They have also another kind of fresh fish that resembles the cod of Newfoundland, and is likewise disposed of at a very low price.

Fresh-water fish, as carp, &c. are sold alive in the streets, and the larger sorts are divided and sliced for the accommodation of those who wish to purchase a very small quantity.

Pu-Quà, Canton, Delin.

Dadley. London. Sculp.ᵗ

Publish'd May 4, 1799, by W. Miller, Old Bond Street, London.

PLATE LXXIX

A SOLDIER OF CHU-SAN

Armed with a Matchlock Gun, &c.

The Chinese are supposed to have known the use of fire-arms and gun-powder at a very early period, but since the conquest of that country by the Tartars, the chief expenditure of gunpowder has been in the frequent practice of firing salutes and discharging of fireworks: in the ingenious contrivance of the latter they are eminently skilful.

The army of China is at present very ill disciplined; its strength consists only in its numbers, which would not compensate in the day of battle for their ignorance of military tactics, and want of personal courage.

The general dress of the soldiery is cumbrous, and for the southern provinces almost suffocating, being lined and quilted. At the right side of this figure hangs his cartouch-box, and on the left his sword, with the point forwards. The matchlock is of the rudest workmanship, and has a forked rest near the muzzle.

It must be thought extraordinary that the Chinese government should continue the use of this clumsy weapon, when the ingenuity of the people so well enables them to manufacture muskets equal to those of Europe.

In the back-ground is a military post, having the usual number of soldiers attending it; these are called out by the centinel on the tower, who is beating a gong, to announce the approach of a man of rank, who is entitled to the compliment of a military salute.

London, Published Jan 1. 1824 by W. Millar Old Bond Street.

PLATE LXXX

A BEGGAR WITH A MONKEY

This beggar carries with him a tame monkey, which by its antics (accompanied with the sound of a gong, which the man strikes occasionally, and which is seen depending from his neck) induces many to bestow an alms upon his master.

Pu-Qúa, Cantòn, Delin.

Dadley, London, Sculp.t

Publiſh'd May 4.1799, by W. Miller, Old Bond Street, London.

PLATE LXXXI

VIEW AT YANG-TCHEOU

In the Province of Che-kian

The city of Yang-tcheou (through which the Embassy passed on the 4th of November, 1793), is of the second order, which is known by its termination, *tcheou.*

The chief building in this subject is a sacred Temple, having the two characteristic flags: on the right is seen a monument, a fort, and part of the city walls.

Chinese fortifications are generally constructed in a manner which Europeans would not consider formidable, but they are, nevertheless, proportional to the efforts of the probable assailants, it being more likely they would be employed against the natives in civil warfare, than against a foreign enemy.

On the fore-ground is seen a tower, and another part of the walls. These defences are in some places continued without interruption over the rivers and canals, and thus become fortified bridges. On the last-mentioned tower and wall are soldiers presenting their shields in front of the embrasures, in compliment to the Embassador. This singular mode of salute, when continued along an extensive line of wall, produced an interesting effect.

On the river are seen many travelling vessels, &c.; the nearest was occupied by a Mandarin attending the Embassy.

London Published Dec. 1. 1803 by M. Miller Old Bond Street

PLATE LXXXII

A WOMAN EMBROIDERING

This woman is seated at a bamboo frame, very much resembling in form such as is used in Europe for quilting. The stool is of porcelain, made in the form of a jar. The Chinese are not ignorant of the art of embroidering, though their works of this nature are by no means superior to those of Europeans. They have a method of embossing upon satin, silk, and velvet; working flowers and fantastic figures in twisted threads, separately, and in various stitches, and then sewing them upon the groundwork.

The Persians ascribe the invention of silken stuffs to one of their first monarchs, but it is given with greater justice to the Chinese. The ancients believed that from the country of the SERES, by moderns denominated CHINA, silk was brought into Persia, and from thence into Greece and Italy; although they erred in conceiving it to be a vegetable production.*

Silk-worms are said to be found in some of the Chinese provinces upon wild mulberry-trees; those, however, from which the best silk proceeds, are fed upon the young and tender leaves of such trees as are regularly pruned and cultivated with the nicest attention. The mode of weaving the filaments spun by those insects into a substantial texture, originated with the ingenious natives of China, though it is now very generally known in various distant countries.

* Velleraque ut foliis depectant tenuia Seres.—Virg. Georg. lib. ii. lin. 121.

Pu-Quà, Cantòn.

Dadley, London, Sculpt.

Publish'd May 4, 1799, by W. Miller, Old Bond Street, London.

PLATE LXXXIII

TEMPORARY BUILDING AT TIEN-SIN

Erected for the Reception of the Embassador

On the 13th of October, 1793, the Embassy reached Tien-sin, being then on its route towards Canton.

This building of mats (on the banks of the Un-leang), was constructed by order of the chief Mandarin of the city, for the purpose of complimenting the Embassador, and entertaining him and his suite with refreshments, &c.

The landing-place was decorated with mats, fancifully painted; the chief Magistrate of the district sat in a chair, while the inferior Mandarins stood in a rank on each side to receive his Lordship, had he thought proper to debark.

The entertainment consisted of a profusion of poultry, confectionary, fresh fruits, preserves, jars of wine, &c. &c. all which were distributed among the various barges of the Embassy, which are distinguished by their yellow flags.

W.Alexander fecit.

London. Published Jan. 1.st. 1804. by W.Miller Old Bond Street.

PLATE LXXXIV

A PORTER WITH FIREWOOD

The Chinese porters are a very robust race; they are said to be able to carry an hundred and fifty pounds weight thirty miles a day. Chests of tea, bales of silk, boxes of porcelain, the produce of distant provinces, are conveyed to the city of Canton by these men.

This porter is supposed to be fatigued with his burden of billet-wood, and resting on his arms to take breath.

Wood for fuel is very scarce in China, but the mountains afford great plenty of coal.

Pu-Quà, Cantòn, Delin.

Dadley, London, Sculp.ᵗ

Publiſh'd May 4 1799, by W. Miller. Old Bond Street, London.

PLATE LXXXV

A TRADESMAN

The dress worn by this person is common among the middle class of the people. The jacket without sleeves is of silk, having a collar made from slips of velvet; the stockings are of cotton quilted, with a border of the same, and his shoes are embroidered.

His pipe, pouch, knife, and chopsticks are suspended from a sash; in his right hand is a basket of birds' nests, which he carries for sale to the epicures of China.

These nests are constructed by birds of the swallow kind, and appear to be composed of the fine filaments of certain sea-weeds, cemented to-gether with a gelatinous substance collected from the rocks and stones on the sea-shore. They are chiefly found in caverns on the islands near the Straits of Sunda, and on an extensive cluster of rocks and islands, called the Paracels, on the coast of Cochin-China.

These nests, when dissolved in water, become a thick jelly, which to a Chinese taste has a most delicious flavour, and communicates, in their opinion, an agreeable taste to whatever food it is combined with. They are therefore highly prized by the upper ranks, and their great expence excludes their use among the poor.

On the bank near which he stands, is a post to which a lantern is attached; the back ground is a scene at Han-tcheou-foo.

W. Alexander fecit.

London Published Nov.ʳ 1.ˢᵗ by W. Miller Old Bond Street.

PLATE LXXXVI

A FURRIER

He offers for sale slips of fur, with which the Chinese in winter make capes and cuffs to their dresses. The tail of a racoon, or some such animal, is often seen hanging as an ornament from their cap. In the depth of winter, the Chinese wear an upper garment, which is lined throughout with the skin of some beast, and, when in wet weather they turn the hairy side outwards, they exhibit a very grotesque appearance. The forests of China are said to abound in almost every species of wild animal; some furs are brought from Siberia and Chinese Tartary; but that of the sea-otter, acquired of late years from the north-west coast of America, is justly held in the highest estimation. It affords the warmth of wool, whilst it rivals the finest unwrought silk in softness and in lustre.

This man wears an article of dress not hitherto described, which is a pocket. The Chinese carry only one, and it is usually concealed by their upper garment; this is separate from their dress, being worn in front, and fastened by strings round the waist.

Pu-Quá, Canton, Delin.

Dadley, London, Sculp.

Publiſh'd May 4 1799, by W. Miller, Old Bond Street, London.

PLATE LXXXVII

A FUNERAL PROCESSION

The leader of this solemn pageant is a priest, who carries a lighted match, with tin-foil and crackers, to which he sets fire when passing a temple or other building for sacred purposes. Four musicians with gongs, flutes, and trumpets follow next; then comes two persons with banners of variegated silk, on the tops of which two lanterns are suspended; these are followed by two mourners clad in loose gowns, and caps of coarse canvas; next to these is the nearest relative, overwhelmed with grief, dressed in the same humble garments, and is prevented from tearing his dishevelled hair by two supporters, who affect to have much ado to keep the frantic mourner from laying violent hands on himself; then follows the corpse, in an uncovered coffin, of very thick wood varnished, on which a tray is placed, containing some viands as offerings; over the coffin is a gay ornamented canopy carried by four men; and lastly, in an open carriage, three females with dejected countenances, arrayed in white, their hair loose, and fillets across their foreheads.

Contrary to European ideas, which comsider white as the symbol of joy, and use it at nuptial celebrations, it is in China the emblem of mourning, and expressive of sorrow.

The scene is at Macao: in the fore ground is a large stone with a monumental inscription; in the distance is seen the inner harbour, and the flag staves of a bonzes' temple.

W. Alexander del.

London Published Nov.r 1.st 1804, by M.r Miller Old Bond Street.

PLATE LXXXVIII

A SERPENT-CATCHER

In China, as in other parts of Asia, there are persons who earn a livelihood by catching serpents. These men have a knack of slipping their hands along the body in a very gentle manner, so as not to alarm the animal, until they reach close behind the head, when, by a sudden compression, they deprive it of any power to escape or injure. The poison and fangs are then taken out, and the serpent is put into a small kind of basket, which the serpent-catcher carries at his girdle.

Canton, Delin.

Dadley, London, Sculp.

Publish'd May 4,1799, by W. Miller, Old Bond Street, London.

PLATE LXXXIX

A STONE BUILDING

in the Form of a Vessel

In one of the courts of the hotel, appointed for the residence of the Embassador in Pekin, was an edifice representing a covered barge; the hull was of hewn stone, situated in a hollow or pond that was filled with water, which was supplied from time to time by buckets from a neighbouring well, as might be necessary; the upper part of this whimsical building was used by part of the suite of the Embassy as a dining room.

The fragments of rocks artificially piled on each other with flower-pots, containing dwarf trees here and there interspersed, will convey in some degree an idea of Chinese taste in ornamental gardening on a small scale.

Over the roof of the stone vessel, and above the wall enclosing this extensive mansion, the tops of a few pagodas, a triumphal arch, and other public buildings were visible within the walls of the great city of Pekin.

This great mansion was built by a late (Hoppo or) collector of customs at Canton, from which situation he was promoted to the collectorship of salt duties at Tien-sien; but his frauds and extortions being here detected, the whole of his immense wealth was confiscated to the crown.

London, Published Nov.ʳ 1ˢᵗ 1804 by W.ᵐ Miller Old Bond Street.

W. Alexander, fecit

PLATE XC

A MILLER

The mill is on a very simple construction, consisting of a round stone table, upon which a mill-stone is placed horizontally; this being turned round breaks the corn with its weight. The man who turns the stone walks backwards.

Pu-Qua, Canton, Delin.

Dadley, London, Sculp.

Publish'd May 4 1799, by W. Miller, Old Bond Street, London.

PLATE XCI

A FISHERMAN AND HIS FAMILY

regaling in their Boat

The female of the group, surrounded by her children, is smoking her pipe. One of these has a gourd fastened to its shoulders, intended to preserve it from drowning, in the event of its falling overboard.

The whole family sleep under the circular mats, which also serve as a cover to retreat to in bad weather; through the roof is a pole, surmounted by a lantern, and on the flag are depicted some Chinese characters.

On the gunwale are three of the leutze, or fishing corvorants of China; in size, they are nearly as large as the goose, and are very strongly formed both in their beak, their legs, and webbed feet. On the lakes of China, immense numbers of rafts and small boats are frequently seen employed in this kind of fishery. A well-trained bird, at a signal from its master, immediately plunges into the water, and soon returns with its prey to the boat to which it belongs; sometimes it encounters a larger fish than it can well manage, in which case the owner goes to assist in the capture; it is said indeed, that these birds have the sagacity to help each other.

That the young leutzes may not gorge their prey, a ring is put on their neck to prevent its passing into the stomach; when they have taken enough to satisfy their master the ring is taken off, and they are then allowed to fish for themselves.

Beyond the boat is a sluice, or flood-gate, for the passage of vessels. The distances behind indicate the serpentine direction of the canal.

W. Alexander Fecit.

London. Published Nov.r 1. 1804. by W.r Miller Old Bond Street.

PLATE XCII

A VIPER-SELLER

There are many different kinds of serpents which the Chinese take medicinally, or for food. The viper, in particular, is conveyed about for sale in baskets, tubs, or jars, either alive or made into broth. The characters on the small board carried by the figure in this plate are highly recommendatory of the virtues of the reptiles beneath.

It is a custom with stationary traders to place on one side, without the door of their shop, a long board of this sort, bearing black or gilt characters upon a red ground, which denote the articles to be disposed within, and the master's name, to which the words "Pu-Hu," 'he will not cheat you,' are frequently subjoined.

u-Quà, Canton, Delin.   Dadley, London, Sculp.ᵗ

Publish'd May 4 1799 by W. Miller, Old Bond Str. London.

PLATE XCIII

EXAMINATION OF A CULPRIT

Before a Mandarin

This subject represents a Female, charged with prostitution. Such an offender is generally punished publicly, by numerous blows with the pan-tsee, or bamboo; and, in cases of notorious infamy, is doomed to suffer the additional sentence of bearing the can-gue; sometimes, however, corporal punishment is commuted into a pecuniary fine.

The Magistrate, habited in full dress, is known to be of royal blood, by the circular badge on his breast, that worn by every other Mandarin being square. The Secretary, who is taking minutes of the proceedings, wears on his girdle his handkerchief and purses, together with a case containing his knife and chopsticks. These purses are merely for ornament, not being made to open.

The Chinese write with a hair pencil and Indian ink: the pencil is held vertically, and the letters are arranged in perpendicular lines from the top of the page to the bottom, beginning at the right and ending on the left side of the paper. The cap worn by the officer of police is distinguished by certain letters which denote the name of the Mandarin he serves.

The manner in which the prisoner is presented is characteristic of the insolence of office and harshness which (even female) delinquents are subject to in that country.

W. Alexander del. feit.

London Published Jan. 1.st 1804 by W. C. Miller Old Bond Street

PLATE XCIV

A SHOEMAKER

This man is making shoes for Europeans, and using very different materials than if working for his countrymen. The Chinese shoemaker works with an awl, and much in the same manner as the European. Instead of an apron, he lays a loose piece of leather across his lap.

It is said that the soles of shoes made in China are very strong, and remarkably durable: but the leather has certainly not the appearance of being cured in a superior manner to that of any other country.

hia. Cantin. Delin.

Dadley. London. Sculp.

Publifhd May 4.1799. by W. Miller. Old Bond Street. London.

PLATE XCV

A PEASANT

With his Wife and Family

Smoking tobacco is so universally prevalent in China, that it is not unusual to see girls of only twelve years of age enjoying this recreation. The Mother is in the dress of the northern provinces; the peak on her forehead is of velvet, and adorned with a bead of agate or glass. The hair is combed back so smooth by the assistance of oil, that it more resembles japan than hair; on the back of her head is a loop of leather, and the whole is kept together by bodkins of ivory or tortoise-shell. The general dress of this class of people male or female is nankeen dyed of various colours, though blue or black is most commonly worn.

The usual method of carrying infants, by mothers who are employed in any manufacture, or at any manual labour, as sculling of boats, &c. is by attaching them to the back in a kind of bag. Sometimes two children are seen fastened at the shoulders in the same manner. The Father wears appended from his girdle, a tobacco purse, knife case, and his flint and steel, by which the Chinese light a pipe very expeditiously. The elder Girl has her hair twisted into a hard knob at the crown, and ornamented with artificial flowers, she is prepared for dinner, having her bowl of rice by her, and her chopsticks in her hand. The feet of children are prevented from growing larger, by hard bandages bound strongly round them, the four smaller toes are turned under the foot, closely compressed, and the great toe forms the point. In consequence of this extraordinary custom the feet of adult women seldom exceed five inches and a half; even the peasantry pique themselves on the smallness of their feet, and take great care to adorn them with embroidered silk shoes, and bands for the ankles, while the rest of their habiliments display the most abject poverty.

W. Alexander fecit.

London Publish'd, July 20. 1797. by G. Nicol. Pall mall.

PLATE XCVI

A COTTON CLEARER

This represents a contrivance in great use for the purpose of clearing cotton from the seeds. By striking, with a small mallet, the catgut string that is attached to the piece of wood which the man holds in his left hand, and to which is affixed a line depending from an elastic piece of bamboo, fastened to his back, he loosens the cotton, and thus, by means of the jarring motion, causes the seeds, or any extraneous substances, to be shaken out of it.

Cotton grows in China in great abundance. The best sort comes from a fruit not very unlike a common apple, which, when perfectly ripe, opens, and discovers the wool.

u Quà. Canton, Delin.

Dadley. London. Sculp.t

Publish'd May 1.1799. by W. Miller, Old Bond Street, London.

PLATE XCVII

A BASKET-WEAVER

Some of the mountains in China produce a remarkable osier, or willow, about the thickness of a man's finger. It is a creeping plant, trailing itself upon the ground, and shooting forth very long sprigs resembling cords. This being very pliable and tough, serves for making cables and other ropes, and when split into thin slips it is wrought into baskets; the method of weaving appears to resemble that practised in Europe. The Chinese excel in manufacturing the wicker-work, the baskets being so closely woven as to serve occasionally for water-buckets.

Pu-Quà, Cantòn, Delin.

Dadley, London, Sculp.

Publiſh'd May 4, 1799, by W. Miller, Old Bond Strt London.

PLATE XCVIII

A FISHERMAN WITH A SCOOP

This Plate exhibits a fisherman who walks into the water, and with his long scoop takes a species of small fish that is found in the mud. Depending from his left side by his handkerchief, is an article of comfort, universally carried by the lower orders in China. It is a small leather pouch, made somewhat like an European pocket-book, to fold over and fasten with a little hook, and may be called a tinder case. Within there is a flint, and a sort of dried fungus by way of tinder, and to the edge or bottom of it is fastened a piece of steel; with these materials, fire is readily procured either to light a pipe or for other uses.

Pu-Qua, Canton, Delin.

Dadley, London, Sculp.t

Publish'd May 4. 1799. by W. Miller, Old Bond Street, London.

PLATE XCIX

A CAP-MAKER

This picture represents the mode of making up that kind of covering which the superior orders of the Chinese wear on their heads in summer. The cap is made of the thinnest rattan slightly woven. The hair which is placed on it for ornament is very fine and light; it grows on the belly of a certain species of cow, and is dyed for this purpose of a beautiful red colour. The demand for these caps is so great, that a single shop is said to have disposed of a thousand in one morning. In court mournings it is customary to take off the red tuft, and to wear the cap without it for twenty-seven days.

P. Qua, Canton, Delin.

Dadley, London, Sculp.

Publish'd May 4.1799, by W. Miller, Old Bond Street, London.

PLATE C

A FEMALE PEASANT

It may be considered as no small alleviation to the anguish of poverty, that peasants in all countries are blest with more perfect use of their limbs than the generality of their superiors—enfeebled by voluptuous indolence. This is more particularly the situation of a poor Chinese female, whose meanness of condition is stamped by the appearance of her full-formed feet, a mark of vulgarity which even a tradesman's daughter would feel miserable to display. In the summer months the young female poor do not wear shoes, stockings, or indeed any article of clothing, except a single garment with long sleeves; and they earn their slender livelihood by hard labour and unpleasing employs. The one represented in this plate is carrying compost in wooden pails for the use of the husbandman or the gardener.

Upon the rivers in China these poor females are constantly seen tugging at the oar, innumerable boats being rowed, or rather sculled, solely by them. It is said there are married women to be found in some of the Chinese provinces, who are so robust and tractable as to drag a plough or cart in harness, whilst the Asiatic husband contents himself with conducting it through the mire.

Quà, Cantòn, Delin.

Dadley, London, Sculp.

Publiſh'd May 4, 1799, by W. Miller, Old Bond Strt. London.

PLATE CI

CANISTER-MAKER

This figure is busied with the soldering-iron, seaming a leaden canister. When the tea is throughly dried, the Chinese put the best sort into these canisters, the tops of which are closely and neatly covered with coloured paper, bearing characters which denote the name and quality of their contents.

Qua, Canton, Delin.   Dadley, London, Sculp.ᵗ

Publish'd May 4. 1799. by W. Miller, Old Bond Strᵗ London.

PLATE CII

A BOY WITH VEGETABLES

The very meaner sort of Chinese subsist principally upon vegetables, roots, and rice. Those of better condition indulge in rich soups, particularly such as are made of birds-nests,* and in highly-seasoned food, which are served up and eaten after a manner peculiar to that country. Their meat is always cut into little pieces, and brought to table in small basins. Instead of salt-cellars small saucers are placed, containing brine or soy, into which they dip their meat. The table-equipage of the Chinese is very sparing, as they do not make use of either table-clothes, plates, spoons, knives, or forks; it consists solely of the basins and saucers above-mentioned, which are placed upon low tables most highly varnished. They take up solids and vegetables with their "Quoit-zau"—'chopsticks,'† which they manage with great dexterity.

In China they have a great variety of indigenous vegetables, also many which are found in Europe. Their kitchen gardens are kept in the highest order, and neither labour nor attention is spared in their cultivation.

---

* These edible nests are formed by a bird which, from its shape and manner of flying, may be classed with the genus Hirundo—the swallow tribe. They are brought from cliffs in the Straits of Sunda, from the coast of Cochin-China, and from caverns on the island of Java, where the Malay people collect them from tremendous precipices, at the immediate hazard of their existence. When thoroughly prepared and purified, they are put into jars, and sold in the principal druggists' shops at a very considerable price. In this state they have somewhat the appearance of isinglass, and which they would probably resemble in tastelessness, but for the plentiful admixture of cinnamon and other spices when served up to table.

† So called by the English, and perhaps originally thus interpreted by some of our common people, either on account of their being appropriated solely to the use of the mouth, or taking up the small pieces of meat. They are very neatly made of ivory, or of ebony tipped with ivory, and usually carried in a small case which hangs from the side. At table they are held betwixt the thumb and two first fingers of the right hand.

-Qua, Canton, Delin.

Dadley. London, Sculp.t

Publish'd May 1.1799. by W. Miller, Old Bond Str.t London.

PLATE CIII

AN OLD MAN POLISHING CRYSTALS

In the northern parts of China there are mountains which afford a very fair species of crystal; of this the Chinese make buttons, seals, and also spectacles; powder of the same being used in polishing and in cutting them.

Pu-Qua, Canton, Delin.

Dadley, London, Sculp.

Publish'd May 4, 1799, by W. Miller, Old Bond Str. London.

PLATE CIV

A BOSCHEE

A Boschee is one of the numerous attendants that precede a mandarin of considerable distinction when he goes abroad.* It is his employment to make room for the retinue to pass, which he effects by exercising his staves over those who refuse to give way. There is however, very seldom any occasion for him to proceed to extremities, as he gives notice of approach by striking his staves together, which, producing a sound of authority, generally prepares a passage for the cavalcade without need of further exertions. His girdle serves either as a whip or a cord to chastise or bind offenders.

* A mandarin of justice is empowered to administer it, in a very summary manner, for trivial offences: for which purpose he is generally attended by two, or more, men who carry the *Pan-Tsee*;—a bamboo, fashioned for conveniently bestowing the bastinado.

Pu-Qua, Canton, Delin.

Dadley, London, Sculp.

Publish'd May 4 1799. by W. Miller, Old Bond Str.t London.

PLATE CV

AN OLD WOMAN TWISTING COTTON

This she manages very dexterously, by rolling it on a curved tile placed upon her knee, with the convex side upwards; after which she winds it into small balls for use.

The industry of the Chinese character induces the most feeble of either sex or age to busy themselves in some employment of profit or utility; and this frequently in requital for the support afforded them by the youthful and robust, who not only protect those advanced in years, but also constantly assign them the most distinguished place and precedence.

Pu-Qua, Canton, Delin.

Dadley, London, Sculp.t

Publish'd May 4 1799, by W. Miller, Old Bond Str.t London.

PLATE CVI

A SOLDIER

The Chinese soldier never wears his full uniform but when he is upon particular duty. His undress consists of a pair of wide drawers squeezed into boots, or stockings of quilted cotton. An under garment of blue or black cotton hangs loosely over them. The jacket is short, made of nankin cloth, and bordered with red; in the centre of this, immediately below the shoulders, is a badge or patch of red cloth, with black characters denoting his company and corps. A long queue hangs down below the waist, and upon the head is worn the small cap covered with red hair.—The full dress uniform consists of a large tunic, weighty with embroidery; this is girded round the waist with a broad belt, and is fastened in front by an ornamental clasp resembling a jewel.

The offensive weapons of the Chinese are bows and arrows, pikes, sabres, matchlocks, and some few muskets. Cannon of small calibres, and for the most part out of repair, are mounted upon their walls and fortresses. They are deemed very indifferent marksmen with their small arms, and to have little skill in the science of artillery. The bowmen carry their bows ready strung in a half case fastened to the left hip; the quiver, containing generally a dozen arrows, hangs across the back, the feathers appearing over the right shoulder. The swordsmen wear their swords upon the left thigh, the hilt swinging behind; in order to draw these swords, the right hand must be passed behind the back; a mode, which, however it might succeed in an insidious attack, certainly exposes the body to an alert antagonist. Some of their swords are made remarkably long, the hafts of which are formed in proportion so as to admit the gripe of both hands; these are unwieldy, and are chiefly used by the headsmen. Their principal reliance in battle is upon the bowmen, who boast of great strength of arm and dexterity.

The defensive arms are conical iron helmets, and coats of mail very thickly quilted, and a broad shield, in the centre of which is usually painted the head of a grinning tiger.

When off duty, the Chinese soldier has leave to pursue the labours of a mechanic or of a husbandman; a practice which relaxes his proper habits, whilst he retains ideas and a deportment rather adverse to civil occupations. Altogether, the profession of arms in China is respectable and comfortable; the pay, which to every individual is more considerable than the wages of any daily labourer, is regularly issued without the smallest deduction; and the situation of a soldier being held honourable, and affording a permanent provision, there is no necessity for either seductive or compulsory measures to recruit their armies, although their military establishment, even in time of peace, including Tartars, is computed to amount to one million infantry and eight hundred thousand cavalry.

Pa-Qua, Canton, Delin.

Dadley, London, Sculp.

Publish'd May 4.1799, by W. Miller Old Bond Str. London.

PLATE CVII

A LAME BEGGAR

Probably not born so, nor judicially afflicted with this calamity by Heaven in his maturer age; but caused by his own parents, who crippled him designedly, in order that he might become an extraordinary object of pity; this practice being reported (perhaps by Calumny, the genius of distortion) to be not very uncommon with the lowest order of Chinese.

The unpleasant sensation which this object may at first excite will be materially dissipated by the consideration that all instances of natural deformity, be it of limb or feature, are so very rare among the populous nations of the eastern world, as to attract universal astonishment whenever they are presented to the view.

It will be observed that the countenances of the four mendicants represented in this work are particularly characteristic.

In the face of the Beggar with his Dog, misery and low artifice are apparent; in the aspect of the man with a Serpent, reluctance and self-disgust are visible; the features of the Beggar with a Monkey are expressive of softness supplicating compassion; and in the visage of this Cripple, pain and wretchedness are most forcibily delineated.

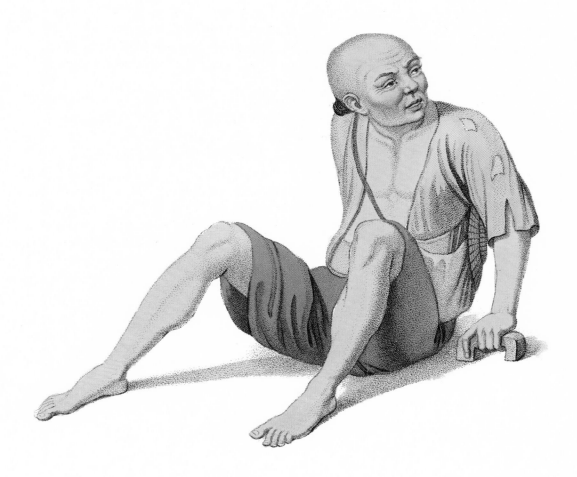

Pa-Qua. Canton. Delin.

Dadley. London. Sculp.

Publifh'd May 4.1799. by W. Miller. Old Bond Str. London.

PLATE CVIII

A LADY OF DISTINCTION

In Her Habit of Ceremony

This is, properly, the figure of a Tartar lady. The women of that country are said to decline imitating their neighbours in the custom of misfashioning their feet; in every other respect—in manners, dress, and features—they accurately resemble the Chinese.

The annexed Plate represents a female of the highest class in her finest habit. The outer dress is of embroidered satin, which is placed upon one of silk; under this they have a kind of waistcoat, and next their persons is worn a silken net. They constantly wear drawers, which are of materials adapted to the season. Their gowns reach almost from the chin to the ground, the long sleeves conceal their hands, and their faces only are perceptible.

Transparent drapery, or clothes fitted exactly to the shape, would be held in China as outrages upon decency; the police of that correct country never tolerating such public exhibitions. The fashions of the Chinese never vary; they are almost of antediluvian invention, and are perhaps emblematic of the stability of their affections.

Those ladies who are advanced in years confine themselves to dresses of the graver colours, such as dark violet or black. A tobacco-pipe and a handkerchief are frequently carried in their hands; with the use of the former they are by no means unacquainted, blending the fumes of that plant with the most fragrant oriental odours. The Chinese women are familiar with the art of painting their skins, using a composition of white and red, which imposes a sort of enamel appearance upon their complexions. They pretend that the latter colour is of a less pernicious quality than what is used in Europe; but we must imagine that their joint association is equally efficacious, with any disguise of the kind, in destroying natural bloom, and inducing premature wrinkles. They do not however adopt factitious charms with any design to allure or to deceive the multitude by concealing the evil condition of their minds or of their bodies. The motive originates from the anxiety to render themselves more excellent in the eyes of one man—that man the sole, acknowledged guardian of their happiness and of their existence. Upon this principle, the solicitous care of a Chinese lady to heighten her natural beauties, becomes in many cases as innocently superfluous as it would be to attempt the brightening of the lustre of a polished gem, or improving the hue and perfume of a rose.

The features of these women are remarkably small and feminine; their eyes emulate the colour and vivacity of those of the antelope. A Chinese has only one wife, but generally as many handmaids to wait upon her as his fortune will support. A state of virtuous widowhood is held in high esteem, and this esteem is secured by her having very little intercourse with society, and by being attended only by domestics of her own sex.

After the manner of other Asiatics, modesty and taciturnity are the peculiar ornaments of Chinese ladies, who are brought up in seclusion and retirement; and who, like many curious flowers, born equally to blush unseen, are reared by their proprietors, come to maturity, fade, and die in their possession.